DAN ZANES'
HOUSE PARTY!

Inspiring | Educating | Creating | Entertaining

Brimming with creative inspiration, how-to projects, and useful information to enrich your everyday life, Quarto Knows is a favorite destination for those pursuing their interests and passions. Visit our site and dig deeper with our books into your area of interest: Quarto Creates, Quarto Cooks, Quarto Homes, Quarto Lives, Quarto Drives, Quarto Explores, Quarto Gifts, or Quarto Kids.

First published in 2018 by Young Voyageur Press, an imprint of The Quarto Group, 401 Second Avenue North, Suite 310, Minneapolis, MN 55401 USA. T (612) 344-8100 F (612) 344-8692 www.QuartoKnows.com

Young Voyageur Press titles are also available at discount for retail, wholesale, promotional, and bulk purchase. For details, contact the Special Sales Manager by email at specialsales@quarto.com or by mail at The Quarto Group, Attn: Special Sales Manager, 401 Second Avenue North, Suite 310, Minneapolis, MN 55401 USA.

10 9 8 7 6 5 4 3 2 1
ISBN: 978-0-7603-6201-3

Library of Congress Cataloging-in-Publication Data is on file.

Acquiring Editor: Dennis Pernu
Project Manager: Alyssa Lochner
Art Director: James Kegley
Cover Designer: Astrid Lewis Reedy
Layout: Amelia LeBarron
Illustrations: Donald Saaf
Music Notation: Claudia Eliaza

Printed in China

DAN ZANES'
HOUSE PARTY!
A FAMILY ROOTS MUSIC TREASURY

BY DAN ZANES
ILLUSTRATIONS BY DONALD SAAF
MUSIC NOTATION BY CLAUDIA ELIAZA
ADDITIONAL NOTATION BY BILLY BUSS

young
voyageur

CONTENTS

A NOTE TO EDUCATORS

Thank you! I've learned so much from you over the years.

I thought that making all-ages music would require many layers, twists, and turns to keep people entertained enough to want to come back for more.

You showed me that I could complicate myself right out of an audience, that young people need to be able to find their way into a song and that there can be beauty in simplicity.

You showed me that to invite young people into the music I should take more cues from James Brown and fewer cues from Genesis—the group, not the book!

You showed me that big themes are certainly not off limits—kids can handle them—but that I needed to find ways to make them accessible. Hitting people over the head doesn't work as well as decorating subjects in wildflowers or burlap, inviting closer inspection, and discussing reactions.

You also showed me the difference between positive encouragement and frustrated pushing. You demonstrated again and again the value of patience and relaxed explanation and exploration. I know I need that too. (I'm trying to learn to speak Haitian Kreyol, so I feel this every day!)

You showed me how to be inspired by the *process* of teaching. That the goal of hearing a group of kids sing sea shanties perfectly (not that perfection and sea shanties are such close companions), for example, isn't the point.

You showed me how to be grateful for the opportunity to work *in any capacity*—parent, teacher, caregiver, neighbor, bandmate—with young people.

You showed me that I might think I'm here to teach, but really I'm learning from young people every day.

Dan Zanes, Brooklyn, NY

BLOW YE WINDS
SONGS OF **WONDER** & **WAVES**

BALLOONS AND ORIGAMI

SOME THOUGHTS ON HOW TO APPROACH THIS BOOK

Thank you for cracking open my songbook. I hope you find it useful in some way or another. I certainly enjoyed putting it together for you!

These songs are ones that I've been singing for quite a while, and although many of them are somewhat ancient, they are by no means hobbling off into the sunset for early retirement. No! They have so much left to give, but they can't do it alone.

There is humanity in these songs. Experience and emotion. Laughter and tears. Stately maturity and unbridled ridiculousness. Who we are and who we might become. The songs tell stories and, at times, seem to say almost nothing at all. But let's not be fooled—there is wisdom in the nonsense too.

Feel free to use this book imperfectly. If we wait to sing songs until we know they will sound just right, we may be waiting a hundred years. The songs can grow with us. Many of them might be a mess at first, but that doesn't always matter. They can be half-remembered with new lyrics added here and there. Some can be tossed around, expanded and contracted, blown up like balloons or folded into swans like pieces of origami.

Many of these songs have religious and spiritual foundations. They ask something of us. They call out for us to open our hearts to each other. To gather in community and to make a joyful noise. There's a difference between "The Welcome Table" and "The Rattlin' Bog." Many songs are wide open to the spontaneous and often irreverent "folk process"—that way of changing and adapting a tune to suit the needs of the occasion—while others require a bit more thought. I can put any nutty thing I want in the nest on the branch of the tree in "The Rattlin' Bog," but when it comes to setting a place at "The Welcome Table," I need to understand and respect the song's cultural and spiritual roots.

As a kid growing up in New Hampshire, I was aware that there was a lot going on in places I'd never seen. I wanted to get out of Concord and be a part of things but I had no idea how that was going to happen, especially as a ten-year-old! Songs were my window to the world outside and they served me well. They still do. They invite me to the party and introduce me to people while I'm there. When the world begins to feel like it's falling apart at the seams, songs remind me of the tremendous power that lies in our ability to share our creativity and voices with one another.

I hope that this songbook, however incomplete, will inspire some singing in your home, school, or workplace and give you what the dozens of songbooks in my bookcases have given me: a sense that we are all connected in this complex world, that there is much to learn, times to listen and times to play, and that this joyful, communal experience we call music making is a way toward full humanity.

ERIE CANAL

Albany to Buffalo. Two weeks on a stagecoach or, after 1825, five days on a canal boat. There was a reason people sang about the Erie Canal: it changed everything! Inland travel opened up and New York City became the American center of commerce.

The first canals were forty feet wide and only four feet deep. As the song suggests, the boats didn't operate with their own power—they were pulled by horses and mules. This was the way they moved until the early twentieth century when boats were able to power themselves. Men who worked on the early canal boats were sometimes called "horse-ocean sailors."

Although "Erie Canal" is usually thought of as a folk song from who-knows-where, it was written by Thomas S. Allen and published in 1905 as a nostalgic pop song about canal life called "Low Bridge, Everybody Down." Tin Pan Alley, baby! ✳

LISTEN . . .

Grand Canal Ballads: History of the Erie Canal

Body, Boots, and Britches: Folk Songs of New York State

Songs of the Horse-Ocean Sailor

all by The Golden Eagle String Band

VISIT . . .

The Erie Canal Museum, Syracuse, New York. It probably won't take you all day, but if you want it to, it could! This beautiful museum has super-solid information and commitment from the people working there.

THE BODY ORCHESTRA

Hand clapping, foot stomping, finger snapping, thigh slapping, hollow-cheek flicking, beatboxing, whistling, chest pounding, humming, tongue clicking, shuffling, lip smacking, and on and on and on . . . there are so many sounds that the body can make. Percussive sounds! Melodic sounds! Festive sounds! Lonesome sounds!

It's easy to get tricked into thinking we need instruments around to make satisfying music, but there are so many sounds that can complement the human voice. Hand clapping is probably the most common accompaniment, but that's just the beginning. Jazz scat singers like Sarah Vaughn, Shooby Taylor, and Jon Hendricks all found ways to use their voices as instruments in unexpected ways. The Golden Gate Quartet would often imitate the sounds of musical instruments in their gospel recordings. Beatboxing exploded on the scene in the 1970s and 1980s but the idea of using the mouth to make percussive sounds was by no means a new one. Using the definition in broad terms, beatboxing is as much of a folk instrument as the fiddle at this point.

Not only are there a million and one sounds that the body can make, there are a million and one ways to interpret a song that can make it memorable, personal, and emotional. Speed it up! Slow it down! Swing harder! Straighten it out! Start out loud and get quiet! And then louder again! And then quiet again! Dynamics, rhythm, and tempo are just some of the ways to liven up the songs. They can sit there like a plant in a pot or they can fly around the room like a sparrow looking for the open window.

ERIE CANAL

With Gusto

Oh, I've got a mule her name is Sal,___ Fif - teen miles on the E - rie Ca - nal.___ She's a good old___ work - er and a good old___ pal, Fif - teen miles on the E - rie Ca - nal.___ We've hauled some barg - es in our___ day, Filled with lum - ber coal, and___ hay. And

we know ev - 'ry inch of the way___ From Al - ba - ny___ to___ Buf___ fa - lo.___ Low Bridge, ev - 'ry - bod - y down, Low bridge, 'cause we're com - ing to a town. And you'll al - ways know your neigh - bor, You'll al - ways know your pal, If you ev - er nav - i - gat - ed on the E - rie Ca - nal!

2 We'd better look around for a job, old gal,
Fifteen miles on the Erie Canal.
You can bet your life I'll never part with
   Sal,
Fifteen miles on the Erie Canal.
Get up there mule, here comes a lock,
We'll make Rome 'bout six o'clock.
One more trip and back we'll go
Right back home to Buffalo.

3 Where would I be if I lost my pal?
Fifteen miles on the Erie Canal.
I'd like to see a mule as good as my Sal,
Fifteen miles on the Erie Canal.
A friend of mine once got her sore,
Now he's got a broken jaw
'Cause she let fly with an iron toe
And kicked him back to Buffalo.

Public Domain, arranged by Dan Zanes. Published by Sister Barbara Music (ASCAP).
From *Rocket Ship Beach* by Dan Zanes and Friends.

PAY ME MY MONEY DOWN

I heard Frankie and Dougie Quimby of the Georgia Sea Island Singers lead this song years ago in New Hampshire. Dougie said it was used by men pulling boats out of the water: "Pay you, you owe me (huh!), pay me my money down (huh!)". Every time Dougie said, "huh!" he would pull on an imaginary rope.

It's been suggested along the way that this song may have originated in the Caribbean, but what we know for sure is that the first published version appeared in 1944 and was from the Georgia Sea Islands. Any music from that region—and there's a lot out there—is inspiring to hear. The area's isolation on the coast of southern Georgia allowed many African traditions to survive during the profound changes of the nineteenth and twentieth centuries.

Many years ago, I was sitting in my daughter's kindergarten class facing twenty kids who wanted to hear another song, but my mind was empty. Suddenly, out of nowhere, "Pay Me My Money Down" appeared in my thoughts! Memories of Frankie and Dougie Quimby surfaced and I sang the song, knowing it would be impossible for these young folks, who had likely never worked a full day in their lives, to understand. But whether or not they understood was beside the point. I never went back to that school without singing this song—it was by far the most requested song in my bag for several years. ✳

LISTEN . . .
Anything by Bessie Jones, Vera Hall, or the Georgia Sea Island Singers.

READ . . .
Slave Songs of the Georgia Sea Islands
by Lydia Parrish

Ain't You Got a Right to the Tree of Life?
by Guy and Candie Carawan

BESSIE JONES

Bessie Jones (1902–1984) worked tirelessly to celebrate and share African American children's music, games, and stories. She grew up in Dawson, Georgia, and eventually settled in St. Simons, a part of the Georgia Sea Islands. There she became the first mainlander to join the Georgia Sea Island Singers, a group dedicated to performing and preserving the music and culture of the region.

Jones began recording with Alan Lomax in the early 1960s and toured as a solo performer and with the Georgia Sea Island Singers. She made many trips to a summer camp in New Hampshire now called Windsor Mountain. I worked in the kitchen there, and although her visits were before my time, her musical legacy was very much alive and well. This is where I learned "Pay Me My Money Down"—yet another example of the ripple effect one person can have when they are on a mission.

I heard Donald Saaf describe Jones' sound as "acoustic James Brown." This is a glorious description for what she could do with her tambourine, voice, and a group clapping and singing along. It's impossible to overstate her abilities as a musician and cultural ambassador.

Vigorously

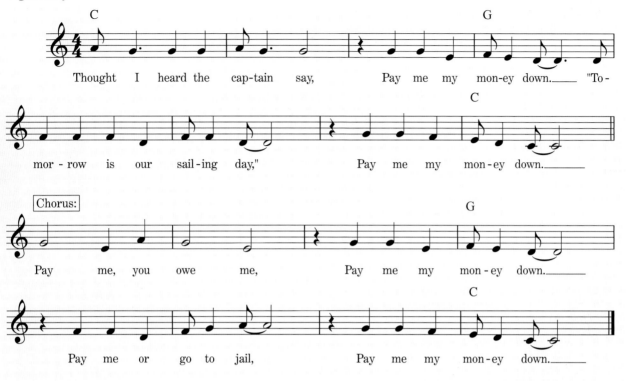

Thought I heard the cap-tain say, Pay me my mon-ey down.___ "To-
mor - row is our sail-ing day," Pay me my mon-ey down.___

Chorus:

Pay me, you owe me, Pay me my mon-ey down.___

Pay me or go to jail, Pay me my mon-ey down.___

2 Late last night we went into a bar
Pay me my money down
They knocked us down with the end of a spar
Pay me my money down.

3 I wish I was Mr. Howard's son
Pay me my money down
Sit in the house and drink good rum
Pay me my money down.

4 Well, I wish I was Mr. Steven's son
Pay me my money down
Sit on the bank and watch the work get done
Pay me my money down.

Traditional, arranged by Dan Zanes.
Published by Sister Barbara Music (ASCAP).
From *Night Time!* by Dan Zanes and Friends.

With Gusto

Pumping Shanty

Aft on the poop deck and walk - ing a - bout,

There's the sec - ond mate so stead - y and so stout.

What he is think - ing of he on - ly knows him - self, We

wish that he would hur - ry up and strike, strike the bell.

Strike the bell, sec - ond mate, let us go be - low.

Look well to wind ward, you can see it's going to blow.

Look at the glass, you can see that it has fell. We

wish that you would hur - ry up and strike, strike the bell!

Traditional, arranged by Dan Zanes. Published by Sister Barbara Music (ASCAP).
From *Sea Music* by Dan Zanes and Friends.

2 Down on the main deck working at the pumps,
There's the starboard watch just longing for
   their bunks.
Over to windward they see a great swell,
They're wishing that the second mate would
   strike, strike the bell.

3 Aft at the wheel poor Anderson stands,
Grasping the spokes in his cold, mittened
   hands.
Looking at the compass head, the course is
   clear and well,
He's wishing that the second mate would
   strike, strike the bell.

4 For'ad in the fo'c'sle head keeping sharp lookout,
There is Johnny standing ready for to shout,
"Lights are burning bright, sir, and everything
   is well!"
He's wishing that the second mate would
   strike, strike the bell.

5 Aft the quarterdeck the gallant captain
   stands,
Looking at the sea with his spy glass in his
   hand.
What he is thinking of we all know very well,
He's thinking more of shortening sail
Then strike, strike the bell.

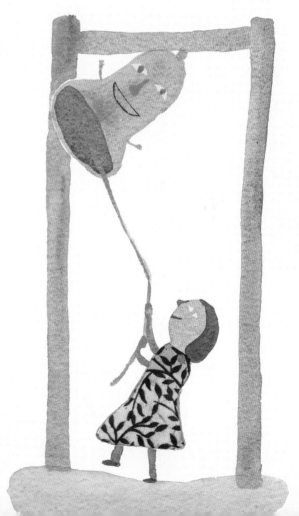

It's going to come up, so we may as well get it out of the way . . . the poop deck is the roof of the cabin located on the rear of the ship's deck.

"Strike the Bell" tells of a system of ringing bells that ruled a sailor's life while at sea. The day was divided into four-hour blocks: work four hours, rest four hours, work four hours, rest four hours, through the day and night. It makes sense that the end of a shift would be great news for the men on deck. This song is told from the point of view of the working sailors who see a storm in the distance. Naturally, they're hoping that the second mate will ring the bell before the winds and rain hit and their jobs become much harder—and wetter! *

LISTEN . . .
"Strike the Bell" from *Two Little Boys: More Old Time Songs for Kids*
by Jeff Warner and Jeff Davis

READ . . .
Roll and Go: Songs of American Sailormen
by Joanna C. Colcord

FAREWELL TO NOVA SCOTIA

With Emotion

The sun was sink-ing down in the West The birds were sing-ing from ev-er-y tree All na-ture seemed to be at rest Still there was no rest for me.

Chorus:

Fare well to No-va Sco-tia Your sea-bound coast May your moun-tains dark and drea-y be For when I'm far a-way On the bri-ney oc-ean tossed Will you ev-er heave a sigh Or a wish for me?

Traditional, arranged by Dan Zanes. Published by Sister Barbara Music (ASCAP).
From *Sea Music* by Dan Zanes and Friends.

2
I grieve to leave my native land
I grieve to leave my comrades all
And my aged loving parents
Whom I always love so dear
And the bonny, bonny lassie that I adore.

3
The drums do beat and the wars do alarm
The captain calls, I must obey
Farewell, farewell to Nova Scotia's charms
For it's early in the morning
And I'm far, far away.

4
I have three brothers they are at rest
Their arms are folded across their chest
But a poor weary sailor the likes of me
Must be tossed and forgotten
In the deep blue sea.

READ . . .

Traditional Songs from Nova Scotia by Helen Creighton

Black Ice: The Lost History of the Colored Hockey League of the Maritimes, 1895–1925 by George and Darril Fosty

LISTEN . . .

Ian & Sylvia. Almost anything by this duo is inspiring.

Gordon Lightfoot. Start with the *Lightfoot!* record and go from there. It's all legendary Canadian folk music.

TRUE HOCKEY HISTORY

Black folks first arrived in Nova Scotia as enslaved people in the eighteenth century. By the early twenty-first century, they represented almost 2.5 percent of the population. It's tempting to look at professional hockey today and say it's not a big sport for black folks, but in 1894 the Colored Hockey League was founded in Nova Scotia with players from the region—twenty-three years before the National Hockey League was formed! It's been said that a player named Eddie Martin of the Halifax Eureka was the first person to use a slap shot, way back in 1906.

I first heard this song while visiting my sister and her husband Donald (the man behind the illustrations in this book) in Guysborough County, Nova Scotia. It was in a tiny old captain's house by the sea, where we used to go hang out in the summer when the kids were still little and touring life wasn't too crazy. I found a cassette tape of bagpipe music behind a couch and felt a need to listen to it. Upon hearing this song, I said, "Let's learn this one. The melody is incredible!" Julia and Donald both said it had been overdone and to let it rest. But I persisted, and we've been playing it ever since.

Canadian artists like Gordon Lightfoot, Ian & Sylvia, and the hard-rocking The Real McKenzies (yes, it sounds great with slamming drums and distorted guitars!) have taken this one on. The Canadian folklorist Helen Creighton recorded a man named Walter Roast singing this song in 1935. She also included it in her book *Traditional Songs from Nova Scotia* as "The Nova Scotia Song." Like most classics, the beauty of the lyrics and the melody comes through no matter how it is sung! ✱

LA SIRENE, LA BALEINE

In the rich, vibrant, and generally misunderstood Haitian religion known as Vodou, La Sirene is the Lwa—or "spirit"—of the water. She resembles a mermaid and is closely linked with La Balen, the whale. La Sirene is often seen with a horn and a mirror.

In this song, the line "Chapo'm tonbe nan la mer" can be loosely translated to mean "My hat fell in the water," although it can be interpreted to relate to another concept more like "My head is in the larger consciousness, a greater knowledge."

The music and culture of Vodou can be found in most aspects of Haitian life. Going back to the '40s and '50s, the sounds of Issa El Saieh and Super Jazz Des Jeunes are an inspired mashup of sacred Vodou folk music and rhythms, American big band jazz, and Afro-Cuban orchestration that could have occurred only in Haiti.

I learned this song from Gaston "Bonga" Jean-Baptiste. He played drums with the groups Foula and Boukman Eksperyans and said that although it can be understood as a mysterious and somewhat funny song that children can easily sing and enjoy, "La Sirene, La Baleine" is best seen as an entry point for anyone wanting to learn more about Vodou. ✳

LISTEN . . .
It's impossible to create a list that even scratches the surface of Haitian music, but here are a few recordings that connect to the writing above.

Saturday Night in Port-Au-Prince by Super Jazz Des Jeunes

Roots of Haiti, Vols. 1–6 by various artists (contains many examples of vodou and rara music)

. . . and anything by Ti Roro (one of Haiti's most legendary drummers), Boukman Eksperyans (who brought racine, or Haitian roots music, to the mainstream), and Issa El Saieh

READ . . .
Divine Horsemen: The Living Gods of Haiti by Maya Deren

Nan Dòmi: An Initiate's Journey into Haitian Vodou by Mimerose Beaubrun

COWBELL
I typically didn't think about the cowbell until the Rolling Stones' "Honky Tonk Women" came on the radio. Of course, I'd dig it, and then forget about cowbells until the next time I heard one.

That was before I heard the Haitian *konpa direk* group DP Express play "M'Pa Pren Contac." Everything about the song grabbed my attention, *especially* the cowbell. It was the funkiest thing I'd ever heard and without a doubt the rhythmic foundation of the tune. I went deeper into *konpa* and sure enough the cowbell was *everywhere!* And it's not just Haiti. Cowbells are common in Cuba, Puerto Rico, Brazil, and Washington, D.C. (A related instrument is the agogô bell, which originated in the Yoruba music of West Africa.)

The idea of hitting a piece of metal with a wooden stick can work easily in many situations. I played in a rock band with a dude who mounted three hubcaps on a frame and banged them with drum sticks. On every single song. It was a great concept at the time, but we may have overused it . . .

Maybe if we had just given him a cowbell, we'd still be playing together!

With Rhythmic Vibrancy

Mwen tap dan - se ak La Si - rene   Cha - po'm ton - be nan lan mer.

M'tap fet - e ak La Si - rene   Cha - po'm ton - be nan lan mer.

Chorus:

La Si - rene,   La Bal - eine,   Cha - po'm ton - be nan lan mer.

La Si - rene,   La Bal - eine,   Cha - po'm ton - be nan lan mer.

2 Tap fete ak La Sirene
Chapo'm tonbe nan la mer.

3 Tap dance ak La Sirene
Chapo'm tonbe nan la mer.

Traditional, arranged by Dan Zanes.
Published by Sister Barbara Music (ASCAP).
From *Little Nut Tree* by Dan Zanes and Friends.

CAPE COD GIRLS

Our man, the scholarly singing sailor Stan Hugill, reports in his classic book *Shanties from the Seven Seas* that this song is also known as "South Australia" and "The Codfish Shanty." A shanty is a work song from the "Golden Age of Sail." One of the exciting things about shanties is that they make great party songs too. Anyone who takes a minute to learn the second and fourth lines of "Cape Cod Girls" will be able to sing half the tune! Those lyrics never change from the verses to the chorus.

The call-and-response nature of this song indicates a strong African influence and, sure enough, in his book *Sea Shanties and Sailor Songs*, Stuart Frank writes, "The practice of shantying on shipboard is descended from West African traditional work songs and was initially a phenomenon of the American and British merchant marines, acquired from black workers in American cotton ports." Frank writes that the period around 1820–1830 was the beginning of shantying as we know it now. Just as we have bluegrass music mostly played by white folks but closely linked to the blues, we also have sea shanties and their undeniable African roots.

Would any sailor two hundred years ago have been able to imagine this work song played on an electric guitar in a room full of dancers? I doubt it, but these days it happens all the time. ✳

LISTEN . . .

Songs of the Tall Ships by The Starboard List

Songs of the Sea: The National Maritime Museum Festival of the Sea by various artists

READ . . .

Black Jacks: African American Seamen in the Age of Sail by W. Jeffrey Bolster

WASHBOARD

The washboard is one of the few instruments that can also be used to clean clothes. Before people were rubbing, tapping, and scraping them with spoons and thimbles to make rhythms, washboards were used *only* for laundry.

The use of the washboard—also known as the rub board—as a musical instrument is believed to have started in Louisiana with zydeco players. Early zydeco bands often created an explosive sound with just an accordion, a triangle, and a washboard. In the 1940s musicians invented the *frottoir*. It has ridges like a washboard and hangs on the shoulders, almost like a bib. The *frottoir* is usually played with bottle openers.

Eventually, blues musicians and jug bands got into the act and began using washboards. The bluesman Washboard Slim attached metal plates, a cowbell, a wood block, and a frying pan to his washboard!

Why play a washboard? They're easy to find! They're versatile! They have a deep past! They look good! They're inexpensive! And they're funky!

2 Cape Cod kids ain't got no sleds . . .
They slide down the dunes on codfish heads . . .

3 Cape Cod doctors ain't got no pills . . .
They give their patients codfish gills . . .

4 Cape Cod cats ain't got no tails . . .
They lost them all in the northeast gales . . .

EXPERIENCE . . .
The Sea Music Festival takes place in early summer at Mystic Seaport in Mystic, Connecticut.

Traditional, arranged by Dan Zanes.
Published by Sister Barbara Music (ASCAP).
From *Sea Music* by Dan Zanes and Friends.

SHENANDOAH

This song helped me discover the wild world of the "sea music" singers in New York. Dedication! Commitment to tradition! Community! Pure gusto! And sometimes . . . ponytails!

I used to take my daughter to hear a group of maritime enthusiasts known as The New York Packet every Sunday afternoon at the South Street Seaport, where they would celebrate music from the Golden Age of Sail (and still do). She would sit listening for hours. I couldn't imagine she would muster that kind of focus if I'd been playing these songs for her at home on the stereo. It was in that unadorned museum lobby with its folding chairs and spirited singing that I learned of the power of live music, particularly in the hearts of young people. There's just no substitute for the real thing.

As far as this song is concerned, it's generally thought that it came from American and Canadian fur traders who traveled by canoe on cold, northern rivers. It's been suggested that the melody they sang was an adaptation of an African American spiritual. Eventually the song made its way to the warm Gulf of Mexico, where deep-sea sailors adopted it as a shanty, or work song. Thus, a North American river shanty became popular with seamen around the world! ✳

LISTEN . . .
Not for Kids Only by David Grisman and Jerry Garcia

Dawg and T by David Grisman and Tony Rice

. . . oh, and Bob Dylan, Harry Belafonte, Suzy Bogguss, Keith Jarrett, and Tom Waits have all recorded this one.

READ . . .
Rise Up Singing: The Group Singing Songbook by Peter Blood and Annie Patterson

12-STRING GUITAR

Most guitars have six strings, but when we talk about guitar music—especially acoustic guitar music—eventually we get to the mighty twelve-string guitar. If you've never seen one up close, just picture a six-string guitar with six *pairs* of strings instead of single strings. Six- and twelve-string guitars have similar body shapes. However, the twelve-string has a bigger sound—and takes twice as long to tune!

Twelve-strings were being sold in the United States by the early twentieth century, but it was sort of a novelty at the time. The person most responsible for popularizing the instrument was Lead Belly, "The King of the 12-String Guitar." The Mexican-American *norteño* singer and player Lydia Mendoza and blues musician Blind Willie McTell, are two other well-known early masters. Although Pete Seeger is generally known as a banjo player, he also worked hard to carry on the legacy of Lead Belly's twelve-string playing after The King died in 1948.

If you listen to my recording of "Shenandoah," you'll hear me playing my Guild twelve-string guitar.

With Feeling

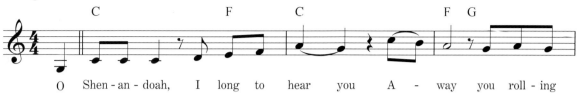

O Shen-an-doah, I long to hear you A - way you roll-ing

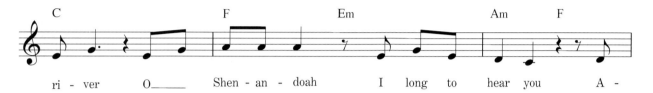

ri - ver O_____ Shen - an - doah I long to hear you A -

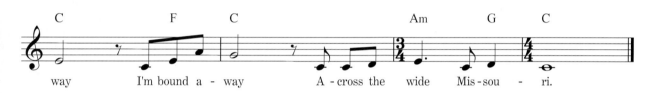

way I'm bound a - way A - cross the wide Mis-sou - ri.

2 The Missouri, she's a mighty river . . .
When she rolls down, her topsails quiver . . .

3 O Shenandoah, I love your daughter . . .
For her I've crossed the rolling water . . . . . .

4 O Shenandoah, I took a notion. . .
To sail across the stormy ocean . . . . . .

5 Seven long years I courted Sally . . .
Seven more I longed to have her . . . . . .

6 Farewell, my dear, I'm bound to leave you . . .
O Shenandoah, I'll not deceive you . . . . . .

Traditional, arranged by Dan Zanes. Published by Sister Barbara Music (ASCAP).
From *Sea Music* by Dan Zanes and Friends

ALL FOR ME GROG

With Spirits

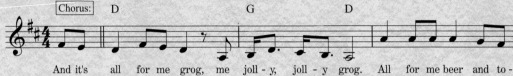

Chorus:

And it's all for me grog, me joll-y, joll-y grog. All for me beer and to-

bac-co. Well I've spent all me tin with the las-sies drink-ing gin Far a-

cross the wes-tern oc-ean I must wan-der. Well, I'm sick in the head and I

have-n't been to bed Since first I came a-shore with me plun-der. I've seen

cen-ti-pedes and snakes And me head is full of aches And I

think I'll make a path for way out yon-der.

Traditional, arranged by Dan Zanes. Published by Sister Barbara Music (ASCAP).
From Sea Music by Dan Zanes and Friends.

2
Where are me boots,
Me noggin', noggin' boots?
They're all sold for beer and tobacco
You see the soles were getting thin
And the uppers letting in
And the heels are looking out for
better weather

3
Where is me shirt,
Me noggin', noggin' shirt?
It's all gone for beer and tobacco
You see the sleeves they got
worn out
And the collar turned about
And the tail is looking out for
better weather.

4
Oh, where is me bed,
Me noggin', noggin' bed?
It's all sold for beer and tobacco
You see I sold it to the girls
And the springs they got all twirls
And the sheets they're looking out
for better weather.

LISTEN . . .

Some lyrics that have been attached to this
song over the years may make you wince, but
songs are here to be adapted with the times:
"Sing at The South Street Seaport"
by X-Seamen's Institute

Irish Drinking Songs by the Clancy Brothers,

Essential Irish Drinking Songs & Sing Alongs
by various artists

English Drinking Songs by A. L. Lloyd

. . . and Louis Killen. Check out his
version of this song—and just about
anything he's recorded.

Some people can drink socially, their laughter with friends enhanced by a moderate amount of "John Barleycorn." That was never me! Maybe I can blame The Clancy Brothers and all those drinking songs I heard as a kid. Whatever the reason there was always chaos that came along with my so-called "good party times."

As I found out later, drinking songs and drinking are two different things. Drinking songs really *are* social. They have all the fun of drinking without the broken furniture and shattered relationships!

The famous Irish folk band the Dubliners had a hit with "All for Me Grog" in the 1960s. Any search for "drinking songs" is likely to lead to a wealth of tunes from England, Scotland, and Ireland. I found much of my cultural identity was wrapped up in these musical traditions. A song called "Fathom the Bowl" helped me understand who my people were and what they did when Saturday night rolled around. ✱

RUM BY ANY OTHER NAME . . .

Grog came from English Admiral Edward Vernon, a.k.a. "Old Groggy," so named for the grogram-style cloak he wore. In 1740, Vernon decided to cut his sailors' daily ration of rum with water.

Boo hoo!

The resulting drink was called "grog." Today, grog can be a term for just about any alcoholic beverage.

TITANIC

This song, which is believed to have originated in the Caribbean, appears in Carl Sandburg's 1927 masterpiece, *The American Songbag*, a book he described as a "ragbag of strips, stripes, and streaks of color from nearly all ends of the earth."

Sandburg was known for his poetry (and later his massive biography of Abraham Lincoln), but music was always a part of his life. As legend goes, he would pull out his guitar at the end of poetry readings and tell people gathered that they could stay or leave, but reading or no reading, he'd be playing tunes around that time of day. Sandburg sang as he wrote, channeling the heart vibrations "out of fun, love, and grief." He became a musician in the days before widespread recorded music, when songs were transmitted from one person to another and regional styles and traditions were common currency.

Sandburg saw music as a way of telling American stories of all kinds, and "Titanic" is a cautionary tale: a ship almost exclusively for rich folks that ultimately sinks in icy waters. I became friendly with the great poet's daughter Helga, who gave me an alternate version of this song that starts with the line "The white folks decided to take a trip . . ." A cautionary tale indeed! ✳

LISTEN . . .

The Great Carl Sandburg: Songs of America by Carl Sandburg

Caribbean Folk Music, Vol. 1 by various artists (compiled by Harold Courlander)

READ . . .

Chicago Poems
Cornhuskers
The American Songbag
all by Carl Sandburg

With a Bounce

The rich folks de-ci-ded to take a trip On the fin-est ship that was ev-er built. The

cap-tain per-suad-ed the peo-ple to think That the Ti-tan-ic too safe to sink.

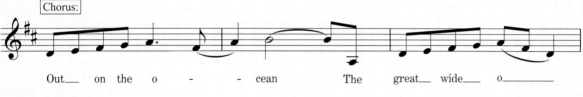

Out___ on the o - - cean The great___ wide___ o_____

o - cean Ti-ta - nic out on the o - cean, Sink-ing down!___

2 The ship left the harbor at a rapid speed,
Carrying everything that people need.
She sailed six hundred miles away,
Met an iceberg in her way.

3 The ship left the harbor, was running fast,
It was her first trip and her last.
Way out on that ocean wide,
An iceberg ripped her in the side.

4 Up comes Bill from the bottom floor,
Said the water was running in the boiler door.
"Go back, Bill, and shut your mouth,
We got forty-eight pumps to keep the water
out!"

5 Just about then the captain looked around,
He saw the *Titanic* was sinking down.
He gave orders to the men around,
"Get your life boats and let them down."

6 The men standing around like heroes brave,
Nothing but the women and the children to save.
The women and the children are wiping their
eyes,
Kissing their husbands and friends good-bye.

7 On the fifteenth day of May nineteen-twelve,
The ship wrecked by an iceberg ocean dwelled.
The people were thinking of Jesus of Nazaree,
While the band played "Nearer My God to
Thee."

Traditional, arranged by Dan Zanes. Published by Sister Barbara Music (ASCAP).
From *Parades and Panoramas: 25 Songs Collected by Carl Sandburg for The American Songbag* by Dan Zanes and Friends.

RED BIRD

SONGS OF DUST & SUNSHINE

WHY A FAMILY BAND?

The music is all around us, in every crack and crevice, in every cloud, behind every curtain. The family band, raggedy and right, can be its mouthpiece and its amplifier turned all the way up. The professionals do their thing day in and day out on the stages of the world, but the family band rocks the frontlines in the living rooms and lunchrooms, the parks and yards, on the boardwalks and stairways.

Songs show us the ways of the world and take us to places previously unknown. They carry us to the other side of the river when no boats appear. Songs bring us visions of peace in tumultuous times. The right songs in the hands of the family band will open doors where none were seen. Family bands carry the candles that scare away the shadows and show us a path forward.

The family band has a song for every occasion and a song to make an occasion out of any event. The songs are in the heads and hearts of the singers, ready and waiting for the moment to arrive. Songs of yesterday and tomorrow. Old and new. Near and far. Songs of laughter, hope, and summer winds.

The family band is in schools and at home. Children! Friends! Teachers! Parents! Neighbors! Gathered on the middle of the bridge where people stop and talk and throw a few pebbles in the water.

The family band needs no stage. The sidewalks and front steps are enough.

The family band needs no instruments. The songs are alive in voices and handclaps.

The family band can last an afternoon or a lifetime.

I hope you find yours.

With Dancing Energy

Fiddle Tune

Did you ev - er go to meet - ing, Un - cle Joe, Un - cle Joe? Did you

ev - er go to meet - ing, Un - cle Joe? Did you

ev - er go to meet - ing, Un - cle Joe, Un - cle Joe? Don't

mind the weath - er if the wind don't blow!

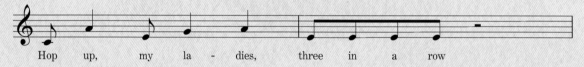

Hop up, my la - dies, three in a row

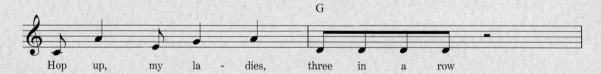

Hop up, my la - dies, three in a row

Hop up, my la - dies, three in a row Don't

mind the weath - er if the wind don't blow!

HOP UP, LADIES

Traditional, arranged by Dan Zanes. Published by Sister Barbara Music (ASCAP).
From *House Party* by Dan Zanes and Friends.

If you're learning to sing basic harmonies and are looking for a good song to practice, here you go! The melody to "Hop Up, Ladies" is generally known as "Miss McLeod's Reel." I don't remember where I learned the version printed here, but I do remember learning another one called "Hop High Ladies, The Cake's All Dough" from the New Lost City Ramblers' *Old-Time String Band Songbook*. They, in turn, based their rendition on a recording by Uncle Dave Macon.

Mike Seeger was a member of the New Lost City Ramblers and from the 1950s through the early twenty-first century was a skilled practitioner of southern mountain music. He was also the son of modernist composer Ruth Crawford Seeger, who wrote a book called *American Folk Songs for Children*, featuring many songs she played at the Washington, D.C., nursery school that Mike and his sister Peggy attended. Pete Seeger, Mike's half-brother, was older and already away at school while this was happening. The roots of American folk music run deep and its branches are wide. The Seeger family is perched on many of them.

"I don't mind the weather so the wind don't blow" is one of the more philosophical lines in old-time music. It is sometimes sung as, "Don't mind the weather if the wind don't blow," or, "Don't mind the weather when the wind don't blow." Whichever way, it contains a deep, positive message for your dancing pleasure. ✱

LISTEN . . .

Old Timey Songs for Children by the New Lost City Ramblers. **The New Lost City Ramblers are sort of one-stop shopping for people looking to find old-time songs without the scratches. The group worked mightily from the 1950s into the twenty-first century to help shine a light on the music and culture of the southern mountains. All their records are satisfying and uplifting.**

READ . . .

A Folksinger's Guide to Grass Roots Harmony by Ethel Raim and Josh Dunson

RUTH CRAWFORD SEEGER

Ruth Crawford Seeger (1901–1953) was a pioneering composer and a crucial figure in the popularization and understanding of folk music in the United States. In the 1920s she studied at the American Conservatory of Music in Chicago, and in 1930 she became the first woman composer to win a Guggenheim Fellowship. A serious modernist, Seeger was also taken very seriously, a rare occurrence at this point in history.

In 1936, Ruth and her husband, Charles Seeger, moved to Washington, D.C., where she worked for the Library of Congress collecting and transcribing folk songs. Her book *American Folk Songs for Children* is still considered a cornerstone text for early-childhood music educators.

Although Ruth Crawford Seeger died of cancer at an early age, her legacy has lived on in the music of her children: Mike, Peggy, and Penny Seeger. They have recorded most of the songs in her songbooks and have carried her love and appreciation for folk music out into the world.

2 Will your horse carry double . . .

3 Is your horse a single-footer . . .

4 Would you rather own a pacer . . .

5 Say, don't you want to gallop . . .

WALTZING MATILDA

Let's start with a short glossary before we get carried away by this beautiful song written in 1895 by Banjo Patterson.

> billabong: a pond created by overflow from a river
>
> billy: a can used to carry and boil water
>
> jumbuck: a sheep
>
> squatter: a landowner
>
> swagman: one who wanders the countryside looking for work (the swag is the bundle of belongings he carries)
>
> trooper: a policeman
>
> waltz Matilda: an Australian slang term meaning "to wander with one's belongings"

So, a wanderer is hanging out by a pond when a sheep comes along. Good news! We can guess that this is a stroke of good luck. He stuffs the sheep in his bag and then—bad news! The landowner appears with three policemen. The wanderer isn't having it, though. This is a free man who's determined to stay free, so he jumps into the water and drowns himself.

This song has been described as the unofficial national anthem of Australia, in part a tribute to the renegade nature of the English convicts who were banished there in the late 1700s and early 1800s. Although the continent's indigenous people had arrived 40,000 to 60,000 years earlier, it was the English settlers who founded the government as it is currently acknowledged.

"Waltzing Matilda" deals with the issue of class. The next step in the musical pathway is a song called "And the Band Played Waltzing Matilda," a hard-hitting antiwar song from the time of World War I that still resonates to this day. ✱

LISTEN . . .

Gurrumul by Gurrumul Yunupingu.

Dr. G. Yunupingu, a.k.a. Gurrumul, was a blind indigenous Australian singer and composer considered during his too-short lifetime to be Australia's most important voice of the century. I heard thirty seconds of this record in a shop in Melbourne and bought a boxful to bring home. This is music that can make people open their hearts and rethink everything they ever learned.

There are several other inspired indigenous musicians from Australia well worth checking out, including Archie Roach, Saltwater Band, Warumpi Band, and Yothu Yindi. Their music is sometimes hard to find but quite worth any time it takes to track down.

With Flair and Flavor

Once a jol - ly swag - man camped by a Bill- a- bong Un-der the shade of a Cool a-bah tree He

sang as he watched and wait-ed 'til his bil -ly boiled "Who'll come a- walt-zing Ma - til -da with me?"

Chorus:

Walt-zing Ma-til - da, Walt-zing Ma-til - da, Who'll come a-walt-zing, Ma - til - da, with me? He

sang as he sat and wait-ed 'til his bil-ly boiled, "Who'll come a-walt-zing Ma - til-da with me?"

2 Down come a jumbuck to drink at the
   water hole,
Up jumped a swagman and grabbed him in glee
And he sang as he stowed him away in his
   tucker bag
"You'll come a-waltzing Matilda with me."

3 Up rode the Squatter a-riding his thoroughbred,
Up rode the Trooper, one, two, three
"Where's that jolly jumbuck you've got in your
   tucker bag?
You'll come a-waltzing Matilda with me."

4 But the swagman he up and jumped
   in the water hole,
Drowning himself by the Coolabah tree
And his ghost may be heard as it sings
   in the Billabong,
"Who'll come a-waltzing Matilda with me?"

Public Domain, arranged by Dan Zanes. Published by Sister Barbara Music (ASCAP).
From *House Party* by Dan Zanes and Friends.

GOING DOWN TO TAMPA

With a Traveling Swing

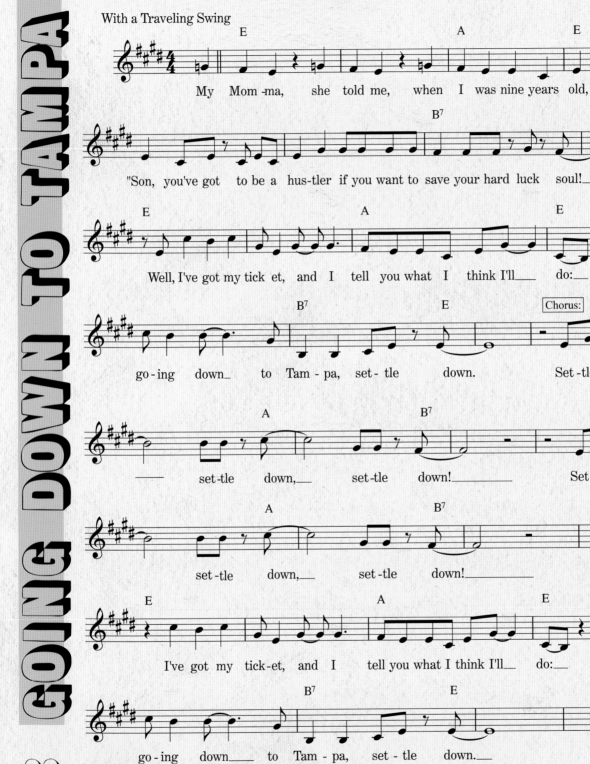

My Mom-ma, she told me, when I was nine years old,

"Son, you've got to be a hus-tler if you want to save your hard luck soul!"

Well, I've got my tick et, and I tell you what I think I'll do: I'm

Chorus:

go-ing down to Tam - pa, set - tle down. Set - tle down,

set -tle down, set -tle down! Set -tle down,

set -tle down, set -tle down!

I've got my tick-et, and I tell you what I think I'll do: I'm

go - ing down to Tam - pa, set - tle down.

Mike Seeger and Paul Brown made a record in 1996 called *Way Down in North Carolina* that included this song. The "settle down, settle down, settle down" chorus was so satisfying I couldn't stop singing it. Where did it come from? As I went back looking for more information, the chorus got smaller and smaller until it disappeared altogether.

James Lowry from Virginia recorded the song in the 1950s and hints at the chorus once and only once—and only a fraction of what Mike Seeger and Paul Brown sang. I went a little further back to the 1940s when Skoodle-Dum-Doo & Sheffield sang "Tampa Blues," but they had no chorus whatsoever! What happened to the chorus I heard Mike Seeger sing? It was gone altogether. I may never know and it doesn't matter anymore. I had gone digging and made some new friends along the way.

When I first tried singing this myself, the verses didn't fit like a glove. I kept some words and left some behind and wrote a few more. I made it something I could relate to: traveling around looking for music . . . the very thing I'd done when I went looking for that chorus! ✳

LISTEN . . .

Virginia Traditions: Western Piedmont Blues by various artists

Rare Country Blues, Vol. 2 (1929–1943) by various artists

READ . . .

Worlds of Sound: The Story of Smithsonian Folkways by Richard Carlin

Black Music by LeRoi James (Amiri Baraka)

2 Conductor, conductor, won't you let me ride your line?
You've got to have a ticket, boy, you know this train ain't mine! I've got my ticket . . .

3 Hollywood, she called me and said there's movies to be made,
I looked around and decided I would find my own parade. I've got my ticket . . .

4 Cleveland in the wintertime, snow up to my head,
Rock and roll was tempting me but I chose sun instead. I've got my ticket . . .

5 Memphis was singing and I thought I'd sing along,
But a voice down in my boots told me it's time to move along. I've got my ticket . . .

6 In Greenville the mariachis played and the future seemed at hand,
Flipped a coin to see if I should go or join the band. I've got my ticket . . .

Traditional, with additional lyrics by Dan Zanes,
arranged by Dan Zanes.
Published by Sister Barbara Music (ASCAP).
From *Little Nut Tree* by Dan Zanes and Friends.

SAIL AWAY, LADIES

In the notes to Volume Two ("Social Music") of his sprawling and mind-boggling 1952 collection, *The Anthology of American Folk Music*, visionary Harry Smith wrote that "Sail Away, Ladies" is "probably similar to much American dance music in the period between the revolutionary and civil wars."

The version Smith includes, a 1926 instrumental solo by a Tennessee fiddler named "Uncle Bunt" Stephens, is the earliest known recording of the song. Track down Uncle Dave Macon & His Fruit Jar Drinkers' version from the following year to experience some highball energy rarely heard in the English-speaking world. For the settlers that made their way across North America in the 1700s and 1800s, the fiddle was the boombox of the day—small, lightweight, portable, and able to get the party started.

On her 1957 album, *At the Gate of Horn*, Odetta completely eliminated the outer edges of folk music with her emotional and driving version of "Sail Away, Ladies," played with an intensity Uncle Bunt could have only found in his dreams.

In other words, this is some flexible and, yes, social music. Play it and sing it as you will. ✱

LISTEN . . .

Anthology of American Folk Music by various artists (compiled by Harry Smith)

Anything by Odetta, especially her live recordings!

READ . . .

Old-Time String Band Songbook (formerly *The New Lost City Ramblers Songbook*) by John Cohen, Mike Seeger, and Hally Wood

ODDS & ENDS

Sometimes it feels like society just wants us to *buy! buy! buy!* It's tempting to think that if we want to make music we need to spend money, but that's just not true.

Every day we throw away one knickknack or another that could be turned into an instrument. Boxes, tin cans, and cartons easily become percussion instruments, but let's not stop there—rubber bands, balloons, walnut shells, buckets, bottle caps, matchboxes, paper plates, whisks, coconut shells, straws, paper towel tubes, funnels, popsicle sticks, jar lids, gourds, cigar boxes, bobby pins, packing tape, and even string can all be used to make music. Even a broken guitar or trumpet or Casio keyboard might be modified to make a sound it was never intended to make.

We often think of homemade instruments as amusements for young people on rainy days, but the world is full of stories of accomplished musicians who built their first instrument from odds and ends. And there are books and blogs galore if you need inspiration. In thirty seconds, you can find plans and ideas for everything from paper plate tambourines to electric kalimbas!

Like music itself, DIY instrument making can be simple, but also limitless. Don't let anyone tell you you can't play songs if you don't have something shiny and new. Unless, of course, it's a bottlecap.

Fiddle Tune Energy

Well, come a - long and go with me   Sail a - way, la - dies, sail a - way

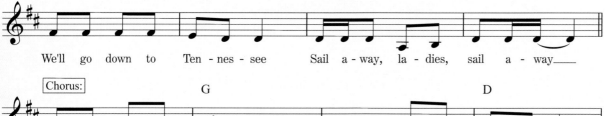

We'll go down to Ten - nes - see   Sail a - way, la - dies, sail a - way___

Chorus:

Don't you rock 'em, dad - dy - o,   Don't you rock 'em dad - dy - o,

Don't you rock 'em Dad - dy - o,   Sail a - way, la - dies, sail a - way.___

2 Ain't no use to sit and cry . . .
   You'll be an angel by and by . . .

3 If I ever get my way . . .
   Tennessee is where I'll stay . . .

4 If I get my new house done . . .
   I'll give the old one to my son . . .

5 Build a house down by the water . . .
   Give the whole thing to my daughter . . .

Traditional, arranged by Dan Zanes & Elizabeth
Mitchell. Published by Sister Barbara Music (ASCAP)
& Last Affair Music (BMI).
From *Turn Turn Turn* by Dan Zanes and Elizabeth
Mitchell with You Are My Flower.

Traditional, arranged by Dan Zanes. Published by Sister Barbara Music (ASCAP).
From *Rocket Ship Beach* by Dan Zanes and Friends.

This is a Jamaican folk song that's been sung in various ways over the years. Many fine versions have been recorded in a style known as "mento," which is a form of rustic Jamaican music that influenced ska and—in spirit, if not sound—reggae. Often confused with calypso, mento peaked in the 1950s before ska captured the nation's ears. (Note that the word "Fe" here translates to "To" in English.)

As a children's song, "Emmanuel Road" is sung while a group sits on the floor in a circle. Singers pass rocks to each other in time with the music. If someone falls behind, the rocks pile up next to them and there is the possibility of fingers getting "mashed."

I learned this song in New York City from a group of Caribbean women known as The Sandy Girls. They talked about singing and playing games by the light of the moon as children back home in Jamaica, Trinidad, and St. Vincent. These women were incredible performers and truly inspired ambassadors for West Indian folk music. They helped me see that our cities and towns are goldmines of vital cultural information that can be recognized and shared once we start talking to each other. ✸

LISTEN . . .
"**Gal and Boy (Emmanuel Road)**" by The Gaylads

"**Hill and Gully Ride; Mandeville Road**" by Lord Composer

"**Emmanuel Road (Gal and Boy)**" by The Two Spars

Mento Mania, Vol. 1 and *Jamaican Mento Music Hits (1952–1958),* both by various artists

Children's Jamaican Songs and Games by Louise Bennett

READ . . .
Reggae Routes: The Story of Jamaican Music by Kevin O'Brien Chang and Wayne H. Chen

MOLE IN THE GROUND

Bascom Lamar Lunsford, the singing, banjo-playing, song-collecting lawyer from North Carolina, recorded this song in 1928. He said he learned it from a neighbor. It later appeared as a part of the *Anthology of American Folk Music* in 1952.

There's a matter-of-fact sense of oddball mystery here that fascinates young folks. How could it not? They deal in mysteries on a daily basis! I heard the all-ages folk singer Tony Saletan make it into a rhyming song—a revelation! He asked people to pick an animal and a place and went out on the limb from there. It works well as a double rhyme. For example: "I wish I was a buzzard in a bed/I wish I was a buzzard in a bed/If I were a buzzard in the bed, I'd hear every word you said/I wish I was a buzzard in a bed."

Or, if the party is rolling along, try it as a triple rhyme: "I wish I was a fly in Dubai/I wish I was a fly in Dubai/If I was a fly in Dubai, I'd give this rhyme another try/I wish I was a fly in Dubai." ✱

LISTEN . . .
Smoky Mountain Ballads by Bascom Lamar Lunsford **(his version of "Jennie Jenkins" is hard to beat)**

Folk Music U.S.A., Vol. 1 by various artists (compiled by Harold Courlander)

READ . . .
The liner notes for any Smithsonian Folkways recordings, including the two mentioned above. There's no label out there that offers this much real information Drink it up!

Banjo Energy

I wish I was a mole in the ground. Yes, I wish I was a mole___ in the ground If I was a mole___ in the ground, I'd root that moun-tain down I wish I was a mole in the ground.

2 Oh, Tippy wants a nine-dollar shawl
Yes, Tippy wants a nine-dollar shawl
When I come o'er the hill with a forty-dollar bill
Baby, where you been so long?

3 I been in the bend so long
Yes, I been in the bend so long
I been in the bend with the rough
   and rowdy men
Baby, where you been so long?

4 Oh, I don't like a railroad man
No, I don't like a railroad man
A railroad man will kill you when he can
And drink up your blood like wine.

5 Oh, I wish I was a lizard in the spring
Yes, I wish I was a lizard in the spring
If I were a lizard in the spring, I'd hear my
   darlin' sing
And I wish I was a lizard in the spring.

6 Oh Capie, let your hair roll down
Capie, let your hair roll down
Let your hair roll down and your bangs
   curl round
Oh Capie, let your hair roll down.

7 I wish I was a mole in the ground
Yes, I wish I was a mole in the ground
If I was a mole in the ground, I'd root that
   mountain down
And I wish I was a mole in the ground.

Traditional, arranged by Dan Zanes. Published by Sister Barbara Music (ASCAP).
From *Rocket Ship Beach* by Dan Zanes and Friends.

ANTA GATA DOKO SA

Medium Tempo Hip Hop Feel

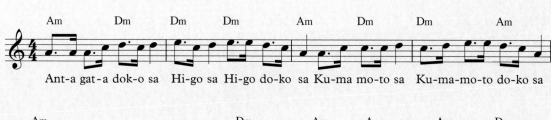

Ant-a gat-a dok-o sa Hi-go sa Hi-go do-ko sa Ku-ma mo-to sa Ku-ma-mo-to do-ko sa

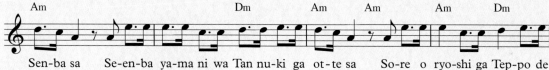

Sen-ba sa Se-en-ba ya-ma ni wa Tan nu-ki ga ot-te sa So-re o ryo-shi ga Tep-po de

ut-te sa Ni-te sa yai-te sa kut-te sa So-re wo ko-no-ha de choi to ka-bu-se_____

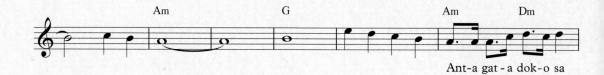

Ant-a gat-a dok-o sa

Brook - lyn sa Brook - lyn do - ko sa New York Ci - ty sa

New York Ci - ty do - ko sa New york sa!

Traditional, arranged by Elena Moon Park. Published by Moonpark Music (ASCAP).
From Rabbit Days and Dumplings by Elena Moon Park and Friends.

TRANSLATION:

Where are you from?
From Higo.
Where in Higo?
In Kumamoto.
Where in Kumamoto?
In Senba.
At Mount Senba
There are tanuki.
Hunters shoot them,
Boil them, grill them, eat them.
Then they cover them with leaves.
Where are you from?
From Brooklyn.
Where is Brooklyn?
In New York City.
Where is New York City?
In New York!

LISTEN . . .

This small list doesn't do justice to the amount of incredible Japanese music at our fingertips, but just for starters . . .

Japanese Folk Music by Shogetsu Watanabe (a classic!)

Vintage Japanese Music, The Modern Enka, Vol. 1 (1950–1951) by various artists **(The other volumes in this series are great too.)**

. . . and music by Utada Hikaru, a modern-day Japanese pop icon with several classic records to choose from. There is also quite a bit of beautiful Japanese children's music available on streaming sites.

READ . . .

Dokkiri! Japanese Indies Music, 1976–1989: A History and Guide by Kato David Hopkins

Japanese Music and Musical Instruments by William P. Malm

Elena Moon Park is a Korean-American fiddle and trumpet player, singer, and song collector. She's taught me numerous songs from East Asia over the years, and this one from Japan is one of my favorites. I'll let her tell the rest:

"'Anta Gata Doko Sa' is a popular Japanese children's song and rhyme, often recited while playing a game with a bouncing ball. The title means 'Where are you from?' The first half of the song is an answer to that question; the second half of the rhyme describes the tanuki, a raccoon-like creature that roams around Mount Senba and is targeted by hunters looking for food.

"There are so many enjoyable things about this song (even if it is sad for the mythical tanuki). The bouncing ball game makes good use of the repeated Japanese word *sa*. In the game, which can be played individually or with a group of friends while singing the rhyme, a player will bounce the ball to the beat, bouncing it under her leg (or to another player) every time the word *sa* appears (which happens a lot, and irregularly!). Also, the first half of the verse, which answers the question 'Where are you from?' can be sung with many different locations in mind. In our version of the song, we included a verse answering the question with 'Brooklyn.' The possibilities are endless!"

Elena's version of "Anta Gata Doko Sa" features New York City–based electronic musician Ikue Mori creating sounds like futuristic bouncing balls and previously unheard-of creatures. ✳

Circus Blues Shuffle

3x Cir - cus came to town and to the cir - cus I went,
I____ car - ried wa - ter for the el - e - phants,
I said to the man____ with the stand - ing up collar,

Did - n't have a tick - et did - n't have a cent.
Back____ and____ forth____ to the well I went,
"Bet____ four____ bits____ that____ ele - phant's hollow."

Cir - cus man said "To see the show with - out a cent, You
Feet____ got sore and my____ back____ got____ bent
Cir - cus man said,____ "First you'll____ see, The

got to car - ry wa - ter for the el - e - phants."
But I could - n't fill up____ the el - e - phants.
an - i - mals in the men - a - ge - rie."

First saw the li - on and the li - on he roared, "A - rrrrrrrr"
Saw the wild cat and the wi - ld cat meowed, "Me - ow"

Saw the wi - ld duck and the wild____ duck quacked, "Quack quack quack"
Saw the old crow and the old crow cawed, "Caw caw caw."

Saw Mis - ter Pos - sum sit - tin' on a limb, big black bear sit - tin' next to him
Saw the hip - po - pot - a - mous splash in the water trying to flirt with the crocodile's daugh - ter.

Saw the old mon - key like in a zoo, and the roo - ster says, "Cock - a - doo - dle - doo."
Saw the gi - raffe and the big kangaroo saw an old Owl____ "Hoo hoo hoo."

Public Domain, arranged by Dan Zanes. Published by Sister Barbara Music (ASCAP).
From *Family Dance* by Dan Zanes and Friends.

WATER FOR THE ELEPHANTS

"Water for the Elephants" was recorded and made popular in the early 1930s by the Indiana blues singer and piano player Leroy Carr and his guitar-playing sidekick Scrapper Blackwell. Leroy Carr had a smooth urban style of singing and was wildly popular with African American audiences. He's not the first name that usually comes up when people talk about blues musicians from that time, but he was, without a doubt, the kingpin of his day and the most influential for several years after his death in 1935. He released over one hundred records and they still sound fresh. Let's pay our respects to Leroy Carr!

Although Leroy Carr had actually worked in a circus as a young man, the song is credited to J. E. Guernsey and Fred Thompson, two white writers who also wrote the B-side to the record, a song called "Papa's on the House Top," another comic blues that is still sung today.

"Water for the Elephants" is social singalong music at its best! The animal names and sounds can go on for loooong stretches of time depending on the imaginations in the room. Most folks don't tend to stick to the script when it comes to this menagerie. ✳

LISTEN . . .
Leroy Carr Complete Recorded Works, Vol. 1–6

. . . and *Popular 1920s Country Ballads* by Vernon Dalhart. **One of country music's early stars, Dalhart also sang some songs by Thompson/Guernsey.**

READ . . .
The Country Blues by Samuel Charters **(includes a solid profile of Leroy Carr)**

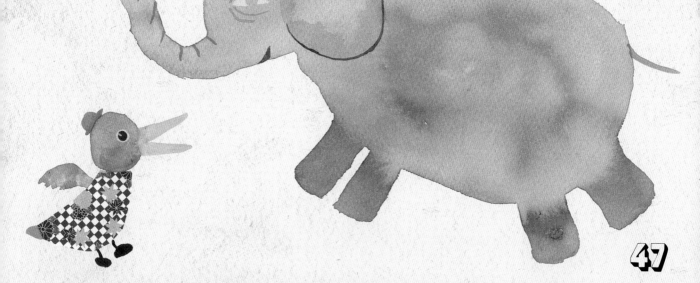

SABO JANE

Traditional, arranged by Dan Zanes. Published by Sister Barbara Music (ASCAP).
From *Little Nut Tree* by Dan Zanes and Friends.

2 Engine gave a crack and the
    whistle gave a squall,
Engineer gone to the hole in the
    wall . . .

3 Winds came down and the river it
    rose,
Cook on the shore just blowing his
    nose . . .

4 I've got a wife and five little
    children,
No more trips on the big
    Macmillan.

Here's a nice day gone wrong! It should have been a pleasant sailing trip with the family on the big Macmillan, but everything started breaking down. If you think about the song "The Titanic," I guess you can't complain too much, but still . . .

As with many of these old-time folk songs, there's some solid philosophy and good advice underneath. In this case it could be summed up like this: when all hell starts to break loose, "there's nothing to do but sit down and sing."

Uncle Dave Macon popularized this song. He said he learned it from African American stevedores on the Cumberland River in the 1880s. Bob Dylan recorded it as "Sarah Jane." Some people have been heard to say it's one of his artistic low points, but I disagree. He was connecting with something old and beautiful, bringing it to a new day, something we all try to do if we're in tune. ✳

READ . . .
Invisible Republic: Bob Dylan's Basement Tapes by Greil Marcus

LISTEN . . .
Old Town School of Folk Music Songbook, Vols. 1–4 by various artists

Ruckus Juice and Chittlins, Vol. 1–2 by various artists. Some of these African American jug band tracks might help a person imagine what "Saro Jane" sounded like when Uncle Dave first heard it.

Good As I Been to You by Bob Dylan

EVENING TIME
SONGS HEARD FROM OPEN WINDOWS

THE SUMMER WIND

I always thought that one of the pleasures of making this family music or all-ages music or social music—or whatever it's called—was the chance to bring songs from the past into the twenty-first century.

The songs don't come into the present day kicking and screaming, either. They take their rightful place, knowing full well that they still have much to offer, in some cases more than ever before. We can abandon the idea that these are dusty old folk songs, relics from the past sitting on a shelf, meant to be taken down occasionally and sung in a certain oldie-days style. These songs have been living and breathing for generations, and when we sing them they will continue to shine a light on who we are and where we're from (and where we might go) for years to come.

The purpose of this book is to introduce you to some new friends or perhaps reintroduce you to some old friends you might have forgotten about. I sometimes think of these songs as books with chapters waiting to be written. Any time a group of people takes them and makes them their own, the songs grow and evolve and rise up, lighting the sky.

We are all music makers—it's a part of the human experience. And yet I've met so many people who have told me that they're "not musical." Maybe they were told along the way that they couldn't (or shouldn't) sing, or maybe they just never found the door that would let them into the experience of music making.

But what does it take? Conditions! The songs, the people, the soup, the sunlight, or the glow of the moon. Whatever the right conditions are for *you*, I hope that this book will help create them and in turn make your life and the lives of the people around you richer and more joyous.

Electronic media has, in many ways, turned us into a nation of consumers. Whatever we want, it's all right there in our hands! But electronic media also gives us a few tools that make it easier to create our own music. I've recorded most of these songs over the years. Those that I haven't recorded I've released by other artists on my label, Festival Five Records. You can easily find and listen to any of them with just a few clicks. In addition to these versions, dozens of others are available and I hope that they inspire you to find the way you like to sing these songs.

WE SHALL NOT BE MOVED

"**I** Shall Not Be Moved," is an African American spiritual based on passages from Jeremiah and Psalms:

"Blessed is the man that trusteth in the Lord, and whose hope the Lord is. For he shall be as a tree planted by the waters . . ." —Jeremiah 17:8–9

"I keep the Lord always before me; because he is at my right hand, I shall not be moved." —Psalms 16:8

In the 1930s, the "I" became "We" when the song was sung by textile workers and coal miners. It quickly became one of the most popular union songs of all time, with the line "The union is behind us, we shall not be moved."

During the Civil Rights era, "We Shall Not Be Moved" took on another new life. In addition to broader lyrics reflecting the struggle, there were verses specific to aspects of the movement. For example:

Our parks are integrating, we shall not be moved . . .
We're sunning on the beaches, we shall not be moved . . .
Tell Governor Wallace, we shall not be moved . . .

According to David Spener's detailed history of this song, entitled *We Shall Not Be Moved/No Nos Moverán*, the first Spanish-language version of the song was sung by striking Mexican pecan shellers in the late 1930s in San Antonio, Texas. In the 1960s, it found renewed popularity with the mostly Mexican and Mexican American United Farm Workers union, as well as the emerging Chicano movement.

And there's more! A young Spanish folk singer named Xesco Boix brought the song to Spain in the 1960s, where it became a part of the movement against the Franco dictatorship. Left-wing freedom fighters in Chile in the 1970s also incorporated "No Nos Moverán" into *their* musical lexicon during protests against the military dictatorship. ✱

READ . . .

We Shall Not Be Moved/No Nos Moverán by David Spener

I Shall Not be Moved by Maya Angelou. **This book, Angelou's fifth poetry collection, isn't specifically about the song, but the message and spirit are important and deserve mention.**

We Shall Not Be Moved: The Jackson Woolworth's Sit-In and the Movement It Inspired by M. J. O'Brien

LISTEN . . .

Rolas de Aztlán: Songs of the Chicano Movement, *Freedom Songs: Selma, Alabama*, and *Classic Labor Songs from Smithsonian Folkways*, all by various artists

The Songs and Stories of Aunt Molly Jackson by Aunt Molly Jackson and John Greenway

With Heart and Emotion

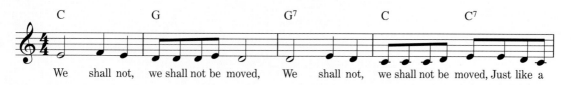

We shall not, we shall not be moved, We shall not, we shall not be moved, Just like a

tree plant-ed by the wa - ter, Oh, we shall not be moved.

2 We're young and old together,
   we shall not be moved . . .

3 We're women and men together,
   we shall not be moved . . .

4 City and country together,
   we shall not be moved . . .

5 We're black and white together,
   we shall not be moved . . .

6 Yes, straight and gay together,
   we shall not be moved . . .

7 We're fighting for our rights,
   we shall not be moved . . .

8 We shall all be free,
   we shall not be moved . . .

9 God is on our side,
   we shall not be moved . . .

Traditional, arranged by Dan Zanes.
Published by Sister Barbara Music (ASCAP).
From *House Party* by Dan Zanes and Friends.

COLÁS

Driving, Hot Weather Energy

Cuan - do yo ten - ia di - ne - ro me de - cian Don Ni - co -

las, Y ahora que ya no ten - go me di - cen Co - lás no

mas. Cuan - do yo ten - ia di - ne - ro me de - cian Don Ni - co -

las, Y ahora que ya no ten - go me di - cen Co - lás no

Chorus:

mas. Co - lás, Co - lás, Co - lás y Ni - co -

las, Lo mu - cho que te quiero y el mal pa - go que me

das. Si quie - res,___ si pue - des___ si no ya lo ver

as, Ay que bo - ni - to bai - la la mu - jer de Ni - co -

las.

Traditional, arranged by Dan Zanes. Published by Sister Barbara Music (ASCAP).
From ¡*Nueva York!* by Dan Zanes and Friends.

2 Bonito el caballo que tiene Nicolas,
Camina pa delante camina para atras.
Bonito el caballo que tiene Nicolas,
Camina pa delante camina para atras.

Ya con esta me despido nos vamos con Colás,
Les dejo en mis canciones un verso de amor y
	paz.
Ya con esta me despido nos vamos con Colás,
Les dejo en mis canciones un verso de amor y
	paz.

"Colás" comes out of the Mexican *son jarocho* tradition, which was the result of Spanish, indigenous, and African cultures intermingling in the coastal state of Veracruz. *Son jarocho* is for the people, by the people (*son* is a song and *jarocho* refers to people from Veracruz). Elements of the music and lifestyle include improvised lyrics, percussive dance, and instrument making. The nylon-stringed *jarana* guitars are essential to the sound, and although they vary in size, they're generally smaller than a typical folk guitar.

Son jarocho gatherings are communal events called *fandangos* and the line between audience and performer is almost nonexistent. In a typical *fandango*, pairs of dancers take turns facing each other on a small hollow wooden platform known as a *tarima* while the musicians sing and play.

Son jarocho has spread to Mexico City, Los Angeles, Nueva York, and beyond. Of course it has! The music is invitational, inclusive, and inspiring. The idea of passing this old-time musical tradition along is central to the spirit of *son jarocho*. ✱

LISTEN . . .

The following are some of the groups playing traditional and modern *son jarocho*. They're calling out for your ears and your feet: Son de Madera, Grupo Mono Blanco, Chuchumbé, Los Cenzontles, Radio Jarocho, **and** Las Cafeteras.

READ . . .

Zarela's Veracruz: Mexico's Simplest Cuisine by Zarela Mertinez and Anne Mendelson. **I know my time traveling through Veracruz was mostly about the music, but what is music without food? And yes, it was unforgettable.**

THE SLOOP JOHN B

Most of the world outside the Bahamas, where this song originated, first learned of "The Sloop John B" in Carl Sandburg's *The American Songbag*. When it appeared on the scene in 1927, it was by far the most multicultural book of its kind. For many, particularly those in academia, this "people's music" wasn't anything to be taken seriously, yet here was a celebrated Chicago poet devoting years of his life to a collection of 280 songs—the book is enormous, and back then it was a big deal!

However limited in scope it may seem by today's standards of folk scholarship, *The American Songbag* let people at last speak for themselves through their music. We've come a long way, and although there's so much more ground to cover and so many more voices to be heard, it feels right to be moving in this direction.

The recorded folk music of the Bahamas is easy to find. If you have singers in your community who know the songs and can belt them out, that's hard to beat. But for most of us, the records will hold the clues. The vocal gospel sound of the sponge-fishing communities is crucial listening, and the guitar playing of Joseph Spence is a trip to a stratosphere previously unknown. *

LISTEN . . .

The Bahamas: Islands of Song and *Kneelin' Down Inside the Gate: The Great Rhyming Singers of the Bahamas,* both by various artists

The Complete Folkways Recordings, 1958 by Joseph Spence

Bahamas 1935: Chanteys and Anthems from Andros and Cat Island by various artists, **recorded by Alan Lomax and Zora Neale Hurston. This has a version of "Sloop John B" called "Histe Up the John B. Sail." It's not exactly the Beach Boys' famous version of this song!**

. . . and anything by Blind Blake, a Bahamian singer and guitar player, not to be confused with Blind Blake, the American blues and ragtime guitar player.

READ . . .

Funky Nassau: Roots, Routes, and Representation in Bahamian Popular Music by Timothy Rommen

Like a Small Ship Rocking

We sailed on the Sloop John B., My grand - fa - ther and me A - round Nas - sau town we____ did roam Drink - ing all night, got in - to a fight I feel so broke up, I want to go home.

2 So hoist up the John B sails
See how the mainsail sets
Call for the captain ashore
Let me go home, let me go home
I want to go home
Well I feel so broke up, I want to go home.

3 The first mate he got drunk
And broke in the people's trunk
Constable come aboard and take him away
Mr. John Stone, please leave me alone
Well I feel so broke up, I want to go home.

4 The cook he got the fits
And threw away all of my grits
Then he went and he ate up all of my corn
Let me go home, let me go home
I want to go home
This is the worst trip, since I've been born.

Traditional, arranged by Dan Zanes. Published by Sister Barbara Music (ASCAP).
From *Sea Music* by Dan Zanes and Friends.

CRAWDAD

This is one of those songs that can easily be adapted to suit most social situations. I feel like I've played it dozens of ways over the past thirty years. Dance party? "Crawdad"! Singalong? "Crawdad"! Lullaby time? "Crawdad" . . . just slow it down!

"Crawdad" has been around for a while. The earliest documented version appeared in folklorist Cecil Sharp's 1917 collection and it's since been adapted along the way. Some variations, including the Music Together adaptation for early childhood, are about simple movements (Everybody up and dance, honey / Everybody shake your pants . . .).

If anybody asks, crawdads are freshwater crustaceans also known as crayfish or crawfish. They look like the lobster's little cousins. Although they're closely associated with Louisiana, crawdads are plentiful in freshwater streams around the United States.

"Sweet Thing," a song from African American traditions, is closely linked to "Crawdad." It's said to have been, once upon a time, a play party song along with another greatest hit for all ages: "Skip to My Lou." ✳

LISTEN . . .

Songs for Little Pickers by Doc Watson

The Watson Family by The Watson Family

JERRY GARCIA AND DAVID GRISMAN

In 1993, Jerry Garcia (1942–1995) and David Grisman (1945–) released a record called *Not for Kids Only*. I was looking for that all-ages sound, and there it was. The songs were old, the spirit was loose, the playing was skillful and soulful, the music was connected to the cultures of the singers, and the harmonies made me think I could do it too.

Everything I loved about the music of Lead Belly, Pete Seeger, and Bessie Jones was in there. The record convinced me that modern-day all-ages music was possible. And my daughter loved it too. At least I think she did. She was one year old when I brought it home and started playing it constantly.

Although a rock star in every sense of the word, Jerry clearly cared deeply about folk traditions and took the time to master them. His band, the Grateful Dead, played for decades, but always pulled the old tunes, sometimes kicking and screaming, into the here and now. They helped a whole generation of scruffy antiestablishment rulebreakers appreciate the music of the very people they were often rebelling against!

But it was when Jerry started rolling tape during jams with mandolin player David Grisman, a.k.a. Dawg, that a new pathway for family music opened. Maybe Jerry and David didn't give it much thought at the time, but the result was groundbreaking all the same. To many rock-and-roll parents looking for a shared musical experience with their kids, one that wasn't particular to the experiences of children—toothbrushes, carseats, bratty brothers—*Not for Kids Only* was something to celebrate, which is exactly what people did.

I should know, I was among them.

Groovy

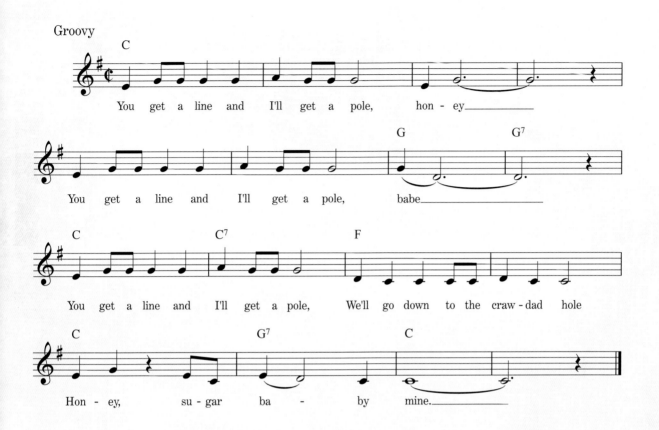

You get a line and I'll get a pole, hon - ey_____

You get a line and I'll get a pole, babe_____

You get a line and I'll get a pole, We'll go down to the craw - dad hole

Hon - ey, su - gar ba - by mine._____

2 Wake up, old man, you slept too late, honey
Wake up, old man, you slept too late, babe
Wake up, old man, you slept too late,
The crawdad girl just passed the gate
Honey, sugar baby mine

3 Yonder comes a man with a sack on
   his back, honey . . .
Packing all the crawdads he can pack . . .

4 What you going to do when the creek
   goes dry, honey . . .
Sit on the banks and watch the
   crawdads die . . .

5 What did the hen say to
   the drake, honey . . .
Ain't no crawdads in that lake . . .

6 Standing on the corner with a dollar in
   my hand, honey . . .
Standing there waiting for the
   crawdad man . . .

Traditional, arranged by Dan Zanes. Published by Sister Barbara Music (ASCAP).
From the book *Hello Hello* by Dan Zanes and Donald Saaf.

WABASH CANNONBALL

Roy Acuff & His Smokey Mountain Boys may have recorded the the version of "The Wabash Cannonball" that landed on the list of "500 Songs That Shaped Rock and Roll," but they certainly weren't the first to sing about this train. This celebration of railroads and musical map of the nation has been a country staple for generations.

Folk singer and labor organizer "Utah" Phillips speaks of the hobo mythology that is embedded in this song. He said the Wabash Cannonball was the last train hobos would ride before going off to the afterlife. Daddy Claxton was one of the well-known hobo figures riding the rails.

It's worth noting that soul singer Percy Sledge and blues artist Blind Willie McTell both recorded this song. Country music was by no means appreciated only by white folks in the mid-twentieth century. ✳

LISTEN . . .

Shine a Light: Field Recordings from the Great American Railroad by Billy Bragg and Joe Henry

Modern Sounds in Country and Western Music by Ray Charles

. . . and anything by the Carter Family, the first family of country music, is going to be satisfying.

READ . . .

Rolling Nowhere: Riding the Rails with America's Hoboes by Ted Conover

Hopping Freight Trains in America by Duffy Littlejohn

Like an Evening Train

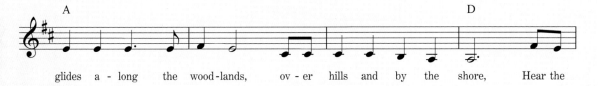

2 From the great Atlantic Ocean to the wide
    Pacific shore,
From the queen of flowing mountains to the
    south belt by the shore,
She's mighty tall and handsome and known
    quite well by all,
She's a modern combination called the Wabash
    Cannonball.

3 Oh, the eastern states are dandy, so the
    western people say,
New York to Chicago and Rock Island
    by the way,
To the hills of Minnesota where the rippling
    waters fall,
No chances can be taken on the Wabash
    Cannonball.

4 Here's to daddy Claxton, may his name
    forever be
Spoken and remembered in the courts of
    Tennessee.
His earthly race is over now, the curtain
    'round him falls,
We'll carry him home to victory on the Wabash
    Cannonball.

5 I have rode the I.C. Limited, also the
    Royal Blue,
Across the eastern countries on the Elkhorn
    number two.
I have rode those highball trains from coast
    to coast, that's all,
But I have found no equal to the Wabash
    Cannonball.

Traditional, arranged by Dan Zanes. Published by Sister Barbara Music (ASCAP).
From *House Party* by Dan Zanes and Friends.

With Joyful Invitation

Traditional, arranged by Dan Zanes. Published by Sister Barbara Music (ASCAP).
From *Little Nut Tree* by Dan Zanes and Friends.

I learned this song from Tareq Abboushi, a Palestinian-American jazz buzuq player, composer, bandleader, and friend. (A *buzuq* is a lute-like instrument with as many as seven strings.) Tareq learned it from Taoufik Ben-Amor, a Tunisian colleague and professor at Columbia University. He, in turn, heard it on a cassette tape from North Africa. Mystery? Beauty? This song has it all! Taoufik suggests that it is North African, probably Moroccan, from the Gnawa tradition.

In an interview with *Afropop Worldwide*, scholar Chouki El Hamel described Gnawa. First, it refers to black North Africans who were originally enslaved in West Africa. Second, it is a mystic order within Islam.

This song has served us well over the years. It's easy to play and has spiritual depth and energy. It can, like the trance music of the Gnawa, go on for quite a while. It gives people something uplifting and healing to sing in a climate that is decidedly anti-Islam. There's power in this song to move hearts and open minds.

I always like to thank Tareq Abboushi for all the work he did in Brooklyn (he's back in Palestine now), turning people on to music from the Arabic world. He's been a strong example of what cultural commitment and generosity (and talent!) look like.

Here's the song: Salaam, Salaam, Asalamu Alaykum/ Asalamu Alaykum befadle Allahe jenaakom/Famathezzo Edaykom wa tee'shoo Zahyeen. And the translation (thank you Rita Farah!): Peace, Peace, Peace Be Upon You/ Peace Be Upon You, and because of God's grace upon you/Don't move your hands and live happily. ✳

READ . . .

Anti-Arab Racism in the USA: Where It Comes from and What It Means for Politics Today by Steven Salaita

Black Morocco: A History of Slavery, Race, and Islam by Chouki El Hamel

LISTEN . . .

Colours of the Night by Mahmoud Guinia

Soirées Gnawa Neurasys Remaster, Vols. 1–12 by Hamid El Kasri

Best of Nass El Ghiwane or Fine Ghadi Biya Khouya by Nass El Ghiwane

Gnawa Home Songs by various artists

One by Shusmo

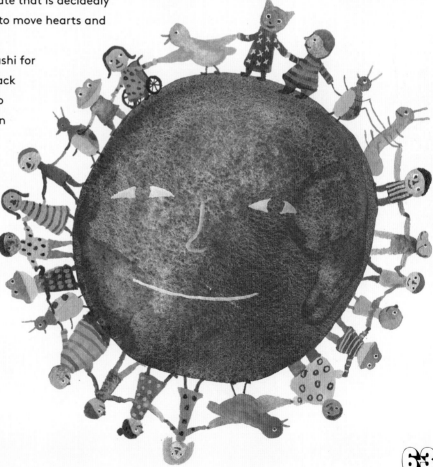

DOWN BY THE RIVERSIDE

In the 1870s, Fisk University, a young and struggling historically black institution, took a financial gamble, pooled the school's meager resources, and sent the Fisk Jubilee Singers on tour to raise money. Although their repertoire included a variety of songs, it was with African American spirituals that they made a name for themselves—and, after months of trial and tribulation, much-needed money for Fisk University.

Up to then, the only other public place a white audience might hear these sacred folk songs—today recognized as some of the world's most enduring music—was in the denigrating atmosphere of a minstrel show.

Later, in the early 1900s, Fisk professor John Work II, attempting to further preserve and elevate black sacred music, revitalized the Fisk Jubilee Singers as a quartet. They recorded a series of songs, including the first recording of "Down by the Riverside," which has since become a celebrated part of American musical life.✱

LISTEN . . .
There Breathes a Hope: The Legacy of John Work II and His Fisk Jubilee Quartet 1909–1916 by Fisk University Jubilee Quartet

READ . . .
The Story of the Jubilee Singers: With Their Songs by J. B. T. Marsh

DR. BERNICE JOHNSON REAGON

I remember clearly the first time I took my daughter to hear Sweet Honey in the Rock's annual children's concert on Dr. Martin Luther King Jr.'s birthday weekend. The lights went low and the audience became silent with expectation.

A single voice came through the sound system singing "This little light of mine . . . I'm going to let it shine. . . ." Other voices slowly joined in and Sweet Honey in the Rock walked gracefully on stage and took their seats. My daughter looked at me and said "Dad, why are you crying?"

The voice of Dr. Bernice Johnson Reagon—Civil Rights activist, writer, song leader, historian, composer, and founder of Sweet Honey in the Rock—had reached that deep emotional place for me and everyone else in the auditorium now joining in with passion, togetherness, and possibility.

Dr. Reagon began singing as a child in the Baptist church in southern Georgia and continued throughout the Civil Rights movement as a member of the Freedom Singers. She grew a reputation as galvanizing song leader and cultural historian.

In addition her extensive work as a researcher and curator (including the multivolume Peabody Award–winning *Wade in the Water* radio series), Dr. Reagon's legacy as a recording artist is one of the most beloved in American music, and paved the way for a new sense of how music can lift spirits, open hearts, advance social justice, and represent the beauty and resilience of the African American community.

And I was crying because I couldn't believe it was possible for something to sound so good.

With Depth and Commitment

I'm going to   lay   down my sword and shield   Down by   the riv - er - side___

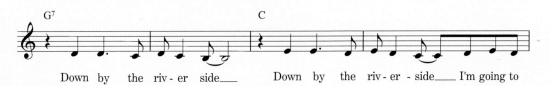

Down by   the riv - er side___   Down by   the riv - er - side___ I'm going to

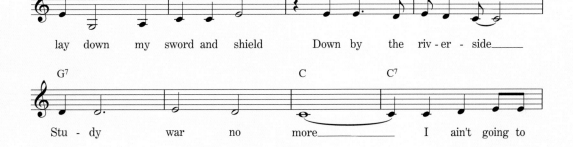

lay down   my sword and shield   Down by   the riv - er - side___

Stu - dy   war   no   more_____   I   ain't going to

Chorus:

stu - dy___ war   no   more   Ain't going to   stu - dy   war   no   more

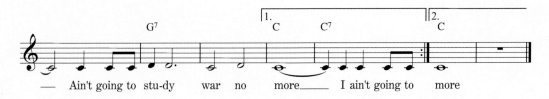

— Ain't going to stu-dy war   no   more___   I ain't going to   more

2 I'm going to lay down my heavy load . . .

3 I'm going to put on my starry crown . . .

4 I'm going to put on my golden shoes . . .

5 I'm going to walk with the Prince of Peace . . .

6 I'm going to shake hands all around the world . . .

Traditional, arranged by Dan Zanes. Published by Sister Barbara Music (ASCAP).
From *Night Time!* **by Dan Zanes and Friends.**

WONDER WHEEL

The Wonder Wheel is a giant Ferris wheel in Brooklyn's Coney Island amusement park. It's about as tall as a fifteen-story building and can be seen for miles. Woody Guthrie wrote about it when he lived in Coney Island. He called it "The Wheel of Life." It's been spinning around since 1920 without a single accident. That's an impressive thing for any ride to brag about.

I went to Coney Island with my daughter's kindergarten class one winter's day. The rides were all closed (it was winter after all!), so we stood on the boardwalk and just looked. Later that night, I wrote this song as I tried to imagine what it might have been like if we'd been able to climb aboard the Wonder Wheel and spin around for awhile.

It's really starting to look like it's not a party until everyone's making hand motions for a song. This is social music. So, here we go, get your hands out and shake them loose: "Round and around," make big circles in the air; "Takes us up," point fingers up; "Takes us down," point fingers down; "I love the sights," hand shading the eyes, gazing in the distance; "I love the sounds," cup hands behind the ears; and "Riding on the Wonder Wheel," more big circles in the air.

It's that simple, but it feels right every time. I like to practice with everybody once—line by line and motion by motion—before jumping in to the song. It helps get some gusto together. ✳

LISTEN . . .
Mermaid Avenue, Vols. 1–3
by Billy Bragg and Wilco

Wonder Wheel by the Klezmatics

READ . . .
My Name is New York: Ramblin'
Around Woody Guthrie's Town
by Nora Guthrie and
the Woody Guthrie Archives

Coney Island: Lost and Found
by Charles Denson

Coney Island Feel

I went to a week-end fair, Met some-one while I was there.
So be-gins an-oth-er day, Cra-zy stops a-long the way.

We put flow-ers in our hair, And rode the Won-der Wheel.
I'll think of fun-ny things to say, And

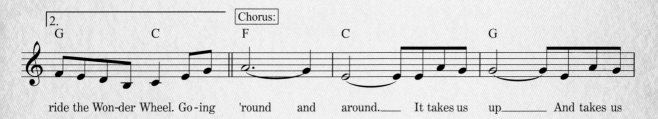

2.
ride the Won-der Wheel. Go-ing 'round and around.___ It takes us up___ And takes us

Chorus:

down.___ I love the sights And I love the sounds, Rid-ing on___ the Won-der Wheel.

2 I looked left and I looked right,
I saw her smile and it was bright.
Like the sun that kind of light,
We're on the Wonder Wheel.

3 Never thought I'd go so high,
Thought I'd laugh until I cried.
I could reach and touch the sky,
We're on the Wonder Wheel.

4 Now the sun is sinking low,
Lights of Coney Island glow.
All the best friends that I know
Are on the Wonder Wheel.

Written by Dan Zanes. Published by Sister Barbara Music (ASCAP).
From *Family Dance* by Dan Zanes and Friends.

SWEET ROSYANNE

This shanty is one of those magical songs that speaks with immediate clarity, and I'm not the only one to think so! I learned it from a recording by Alan Lomax, who collected it from the Bright Light Quartet, a group of African American fishermen in Virginia in 1960.

His words speak to its undeniable power: "We were in Shedrick Cain's front parlor talking over songs when somebody began to hum this tune. It is not often that a song hunter hears a new piece which has the recognizable quality of a new national song. It has happened only a few times in my twenty-eight years of recording, when I heard 'Down in the Valley' in 1933, 'Irene, Goodnight' in 1934, and 'Rock Island Line' in 1938. Here was one of those that all America will be singing someday, I thought."

Anyone can see why he thought that. "Sweet Rosyanne" is magical and simple, a solid combination. I've never heard a version that wasn't emotionally satisfying and at least a little mysterious. It's the American equivalent of the Scottish folk song "The Parting Glass."

The original version is in 3/4 waltz time with a measure of 4/4 in the middle of the chorus. We've smoothed out the extra beat with the hope that it'll be more socially inviting without losing its flavor. And it's easy to find the original version if you want to get that beat back. *

LISTEN . . .

Alan Lomax Southern Journey, Vols. 1–13
by various artists

No conversation about American roots music is complete without a look at the music recorded by Alan Lomax in 1959–1960. Incredible field recordings . . . in stereo!

READ . . .

The Association for Cultural Equity (www.culturalequity.org). How's this for a goal? "Inspired by the example set by Alan Lomax, our mission is to stimulate cultural equity through preservation, research, and dissemination of the world's traditional music, and to reconnect people and communities with their creative heritage." It's a mind-boggling website, so set aside some time!

Slowly and Socially

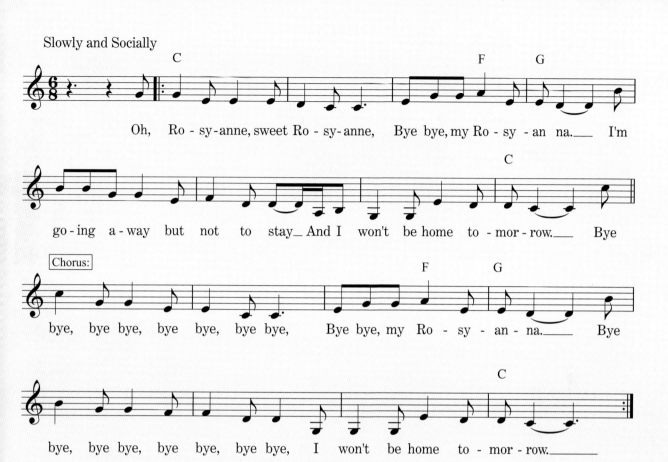

Oh, Ro-sy-anne, sweet Ro-sy-anne, Bye bye, my Ro-sy-an na.___ I'm

go-ing a-way but not to stay___ And I won't be home to-mor-row.___ Bye

Chorus:

bye, bye bye, bye bye, bye bye, Bye bye, my Ro-sy-an-na.___ Bye

bye, bye bye, bye bye, bye bye, I won't be home to-mor-row._____

2 I thought I heard the captain say,
Bye bye, my Rosyanna.
Don't you want to go home on your next
   payday?
I won't be home tomorrow.

3 A dollar a day is a fisherman's pay,
Bye bye, my Rosyanna.
Easy come easy go away,
I won't be home tomorrow.

4 Steamboat's coming around the bend,
Bye bye, my Rosyanna.
She's loaded down with fishermen,
I won't be home tomorrow.

5 Steamboat's coming around the bend,
Bye bye, my Rosyanna.
She's loaded down with harvestmen,
I won't be home tomorrow.

Lawrence Hodge, Arnold Fisher, James Campbell, Robert Beane, Shedrick Caine, Alan Lomax. Ludlow Music, Inc. (BMI).
From *Catch That Train* by Dan Zanes and Friends.

ROLLING HOME

SONGS OF
GUSTO & CELEBRATION

WASP RAMBLINGS

I've learned so much working on this book! What a pleasure it's been to ponder and read and dig and search and listen and develop a deeper understanding of the sixty-four songs you find here. Most of them have been my companions and teachers for many years. They were around when my daughter was born and filled the house while she was growing up. They were guests at many dinners and late-night parties.

These songs have helped me think about history. I thought I knew them well, but in many cases I was wrong. There are a number of songs here that I considered to be from the white southern mountain culture—"Crawdad," "All Around the Kitchen!," and "Saro Jane," for example. But their roots go back to African American musical traditions. In my digging I started to see new narratives and musical pathways.

These songs have helped me think about heritage and identity. Once I knew who I was, where my people came from and what they sang, I started to feel a lot more comfortable in the world. When I was just a "white guy" with no real past that I understood, I felt I had nothing substantial to offer and consequently I was always looking around for good stuff from other cultures. When I could finally see myself for who I really was: a New England WASP (White Anglo-Saxon Protestant) with roots in Britain, Scotland, and Ireland, I had something to share.

These songs have helped me think about feelings. No matter how catchy and singable a tune might be, I didn't include ones that made me (and probably others) uncomfortable. I've recorded "Polly Wolly Doodle" and "Jim Along Josie," but when I discovered their minstrel show roots, I decided to let them gather dust. I wanted to include a sea shanty called "John Kanakanaka" but the term "kanaka," once a reference to Hawai'ians, has become a racial slur Australia used towards Pacific Islanders, so what's the point? If I can sing it comfortably in Woodstock but not in Melbourne then I don't need it. No tune is so great that it can't be ditched it if it's problematic. There are plenty more in the wings and if there aren't, well, I'll write one . . .

These songs have helped me think about currency—what we're able to share with each other. When I have a headful of songs, I can move freely in the world. I learned this when I was seventeen years old hitchhiking through Scotland. I knew a lot of country-and-western and folk songs and as a result I was able to make friends. This situation wouldn't have worked for everyone, but the point is that any of us with a headful of songs for a variety of occasions have something useful to offer. Isn't that what we want—to be useful?

These songs have also helped me think about responsibility. They're there when we need them—if we know they exist. I learned that the more energy I put into finding and learning songs, the more I have to work with when situations call for something musical. If the meal is over and the plates are cleared, that can be a "Country Life" moment. Or an "El Botellón" moment. But if someone doesn't get the singing started, it'll probably be more of a chatter-and-scatter moment. Knowing some songs and being able to get people singing isn't complicated or difficult, but it doesn't always happen on its own. Songs bring us together and songs keep us together and the more of them you know the more you can help make those memorable and often magical moments happen.

SON BORINQUEÑO

With Rhythmic Drive and Flair

Lay lo lo lay lo Lay___ lo lo lay lo Lay___ lo lo lay lo lie.___

Lay lo lo lay lo Lay___ lo lo lay lo Lay___ lo lo lay lo lie.___

Chorus:

Can - ta mi pue - blo, can - ta mi gen - te, Can -

ta en En - er - o, can - ta en Dic - iem - bre,

Can - ta mi pueb - lo, can - ta mi gen - te, Son Bo - rin - queñ - o.

Suen - an___ tam - bor - i - les y bon - gos,

Suen - an___ las mar - a - cas y el tam - bor.

Ya va___ a empezar la fies - ta Suena un___ lo - co

Traditional, arranged by Dan Zanes. Published by Sister Barbara Music (ASCAP).

From ¡*Nueva York!* by Dan Zanes and Friends.

la trom-pe - ta__ Y__ Ne - lly la pan-der-e - ta,__ Nos_ pone - mos a

bai - la bom - ba__ Cuan - do__ ya - yo to - ca con - ga.__

2 Oye, que la fiesta ya empezó. Unos invitados y otros no. Oye ya la algarabía, Y la gente no se cansa, Un tipo pidió una danza, Una señora un danzón, Y mi amigo un guaguancó. Lay lo lo lay lo

LISTEN . . .

15 Aguinaldos Da' Quí Con Ramito by Ramito. **I think all of his recordings are great. And don't forget Chuíto, and Odilio Gonzalez.**

Verdadera Navidad by Quique Domenech. **One of the most heralded of the new generation of cuatro players, and for good reason!**

¡Saoco! The Bomba and Plena Explosion in Puerto Rico 1954–1966 by various artists.

"Son Borinqueño" is an *aguinaldo*, a traditional Puerto Rican song for the Christmas season. This style of holiday folk music is joyful, uplifting, and tremendously rocking. One of the seasonal traditions is the *parranda*, a procession of friends and neighbors who go from house to house with instruments and voices offering songs. It's a like Christmas caroling turned *all the way up.*

Some well-known purveyors of *aguinaldos* are *jibaro* singers. *Jíbaro* music is the mountain folk music that features the ten-string *cuatro* (often referred to as the national instrument of Puerto Rico), guitar, *guiro*, and sometimes other percussion instruments such as bongos, maracas, or congas (hence "tamboriles y bongos" in the song).

The Christmas season in Puerto Rico goes into the early part of January. I've been down there for it and can attest to the unbridled beauty and strong sense of community during those weeks. And the food is amazing.

I learned this song from Bernardo Palombo, an Argentinian singer and composer and the main man behind El Taller Latino Americano, a cultural center and Spanish language school in East Harlem.

Bernardo has helped many of us find our way into the music and life of Latin America. He's an example of the difference cultural generosity can make in a community. The ripple effects are impossible to measure. ✱

73

DANIEL IN THE DEN

This is a short song, but the miracles are packed in here! It includes an amazing cast of characters: Daniel, Moses, Jesus, Jonah, Shadrach, Meshach, and Abednego. It could be said for religious music worldwide, but in the United States it's especially hard to deny the impact of black gospel music on almost every aspect of our culture. Rock and roll, for example. Without black gospel, rock and roll would sound like a broom sweeping the floor.

My brother-in-law Donald Saaf (the illustrator of this book!) taught me this song. He said he learned it from a recording Sister Rosetta Tharpe made with her singing and mandolin-playing mother, Katie Bell Nubin (as "Daniel in the Lion's Den"). People say it's one of the greatest mother-daughter duets of these modern times.

The legacy of Sister Rosetta Tharpe must be considered in a bit more detail. Long before there was a music *called* rock and roll, here was an African American woman *playing* rock and roll. The men generally given credit for "inventing" this music in the 1950s have mostly acknowledged her as the trailblazer. Chuck Berry even referred to his career as "one long Rosetta Tharpe impersonation." She was Little Richard's greatest influence. Elvis spoke frequently about her singing and even more about her guitar playing.

In the decades following her death in 1973, Sister Rosetta Tharpe's legacy was mostly forgotten. However, in recent years she's finally been getting the credit she deserves as (among other things) "The Godmother of Rock and Roll." ✳

LISTEN . . .

Gospel Train by Sister Rosetta Tharpe **(There are many more classics to choose from!)**

The Key to the Kingdom by Washington Phillips

"Daniel in the Lion's Den" by Bessie Jones and the Georgia Sea Island Singers

"Daniel (in the Lion's Den)" by Prince Alla and Junior Reid

READ . . .

The Bible. *The Everyday Life Bible: Amplified Version* with commentary by Joyce Meyer is a solid option.

Shout, Sister, Shout!: The Untold Story of Rock-and-Roll Trailblazer Sister Rosetta Tharpe by Gayle Wald

Power through Constructive Thinking by Emmet Fox. See the chapter titled "Daniel in the Lion's Den." Fox was a wildly popular Christian author and speaker in the '30s and '40s. His work is still read today.

With Pulse and Energy

Dan - iel in the den (in the den) In the den, (in the den) In the lio-n's den

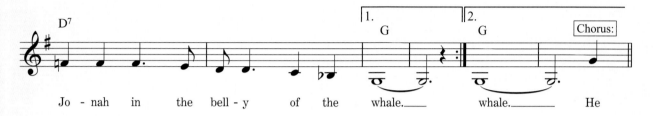

Jo - nah in the bell - y of the whale.___ whale.___ He

1.
G

2.
G

Chorus:

locked the li - on's___ jaw. (he locked) He locked the li - on's___ jaw. (he locked) He

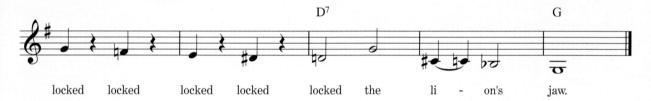

locked locked locked locked locked the li - on's jaw.

D7

G

2 He parted the sea (the sea)
The sea (the sea)
The deep blue sea
To help Moses get across. [2x]

3 Sent down his Son (his Son)
His Son (his Son)
His suffering Son
See what the good
Lord has done. [2x]

4 Shadrach, Meshach, and Abednego
Walked out (walked out)
Walked out of the flames [2x]

Traditional, arranged by Dan Zanes. Published by Sister Barbara Music (ASCAP).
From *The Welcome Table: Songs of Inspiration, Mystery & Good Times* by Dan Zanes and Friends.

75

KING KONG KITCHIE

This is one of many versions of "Froggie Went A-Courting," and what a nice one it is, based on a recording by Chubby Parker.

The origins of the song seem to go back to the late 1500s. A version published in 1611 shows that some things about this story have remained quite constant over the years: Mr. Frog went to see Miss Mouse. He was armed. He wasn't just popping in for a quick hello—he wanted to get married. A few other animals dropped by (a rat is almost always among them; very often, the rat is Miss Mouse's uncle). There was a crazy meal, the kind that you can't really have every day (it wouldn't be healthy to eat, for example, "three beans in a pound of butter" regularly). The song has stayed with us for centuries and while the details may have changed with time, the cosmic foolishness of the story has remained intact.

I first heard Chubby Parker sing this song on *The Anthology of American Folk Music*, a collection put together by the visionary bohemian filmmaker Harry Smith. In the liner notes he wrote this about "King Kong Kitchie": "Zoologic Miscegeny Achieved Mouse Frog Nuptuals [sic], Relatives Approve." And this is just an *average* entry in one of the most forward-thinking and glorious presentations of folk music ever assembled. Smith was an important figure in the Beat Movement, and poet Allen Ginsberg took care of him for many of Harry Smith's final years. ✳

READ . . .

Howl and Other Poems
by Allen Ginsberg

Coney Island of the Mind
by Lawrence Ferlinghetti

Helping the Dreamer: New and Selected Poems 1966–1988
by Anne Waldman

LISTEN . . .

Pieces of a Man by Gil Scott-Heron. **If we're talking about poetry, let's talk about Gil Scott-Heron!**

Laughing in Rhythm: The Best of the Verve Years by Slim Gaillard. **He's some kind of jazzy cousin of Chubby Parker, and certainly a good person to have at any party!**

Like a Horse Trotting

Frog-gie went a court-ing and he did ride, King kong kit-chie kit-chie ki - mee-o. With a

sword and pis - tol by his side, King kong kit-chie kit-chie ki - mee - o.

Chorus:

Ki - mo-kee - mo ki - mo-kee, Way down yon-der in a hol-low tree. An

owl and a bat and a bum-ble bee, King kong kit-chie kit-chie ki - mee - o.

ex. Mandolin or Guitar Fill

2
He rode 'til he came to Miss Mousie's door . . .
And there he knelt upon the floor . . .

3
He took Miss Mouse upon his knee . . .
And he said, "Little mouse, will you marry
me?" . . .

4
Miss Mouse had suitors three or four . . .
And there they came right through the door . . .

5
They grabbed Mr. Frog and began to fight . . .
In the hollow tree it was a terrible night . . .

6
Mr. Frog brought the suitors to the floor . . .
With the sword and the pistol he scared all
four . . .

7
They went to the park on the very next day . . .
And left on their honeymoon right away . . .

8
Now they live far off in a hollow tree . . .
Where they now have wealth and children
three . . .

Traditional, arranged by Dan Zanes. Published by Sister Barbara Music (ASCAP).
From *Rocket Ship Beach* by Dan Zanes and Friends.

THIS LITTLE LIGHT OF MINE

To many people, "This Little Light of Mine" is a children's song. A classic for the preschool crowd. The central role it played in the 1960s Civil Rights Movement, however, is often forgotten. Pete Seeger wrote from Greenwood, Mississippi, in 1963, "The most popular song by all odds was 'This Little Light of Mine, I'm Going to Let It Shine'. I must have heard it sung a dozen times a day, and once it was started it would go on for 10 and 15 and 20 minutes with people singing new words and repeating the old ones."

Fannie Lou Hamer is one of the most inspiring (and underappreciated) figures of the Civil Rights Movement. Her activism started in 1962 with the voter registration drive in Ruleville, Mississippi. She was in her mid-forties and remained a tireless and fearless organizer until her death in 1977 at age fifty-nine. Her grassroots efforts with the Student Nonviolent Coordinating Committee (SNCC) brought her in regular contact with brutal racism. In 1964 she ran for Congress. Although her campaign was unsuccessful, it helped begin increased black representation in Mississippi Democratic Party politics.

Health issues plagued Fannie Lou for much of her life, and although her time as an activist was relatively brief, her impact is felt to this day thanks to her involvement in voter registration drives, the Freedom Summer, the 1964 Democratic Convention, literacy efforts, the Poor People's Campaign, the Freedom Farm Cooperative, the National Council of Negro Women, and the National Women's Political Caucus.

And all along the way she sang. Fannie Lou was a gifted singer who used music to inspire everyone around her in the struggle for equal rights and dignity in the United States. "This Little Light of Mine" was her signature song. ✳

LISTEN . . .

Voices of the Civil Rights Movement: Black American Freedom Songs 1960–1966 by various artists

Fannie Lou Hamer: Songs My Mother Taught Me

The Staple Singers: This Little Light of Mine

READ . . .

Sing for Freedom: The Story of the Civil Rights Movement Through Its Songs (also available as a CD)

We Who Believe in Freedom: Sweet Honey in The Rock . . . Still on the Journey by Bernice Johnson Reagon

WATCH . . .

This Little Light of Mine: The Legacy of Fannie Lou Hamer, directed by Robin N. Hamilton

Eyes on the Prize: America's Civil Rights Movement, 14 episodes produced for PBS by Henry Hampton

With a Driving Energy

2 Everywhere I go . . .

3 In my daily work . . .

4 Out there in the dark . . .

5 In my neighborhood . . .

6 Hide it under a bushel (No!) . . .

7 I've got the light of peace and love . . .

8 I've got the light of freedom . . .

9 All in the jailhouse . . .

Traditional, arranged by Dan Zanes. Published by Sister Barbara Music (ASCAP).

ROCK ISLAND LINE

Lead Belly, the "King of the 12-string guitar," sang a mix of old and new songs from a variety of places—songs always played in his own unique style. He sang songs that immediately spoke to young people and gave them glimpses of a world that was likely unknown to them. I was an eight-year-old in Concord, New Hampshire, when I first heard his music, and it seemed like the curtains to the globe were opened for the first time. His music for children was fun, but it was soulful and meaningful. Lead Belly sang songs that young people could share with grown-ups, songs that they could carry through life.

When I wanted to make a record of the songs that Lead Belly sang for children, I called the Lead Belly family and estate to see how they felt about the project. It was important that I have their blessing. They said, "Go for it!" The narrative of his time in prison is constantly overshadowing his strong emotional connection to young audiences and other aspects of his career. If this distortion is happening with Lead Belly, arguably the greatest folk singer of the twentieth century, where else is it happening in our casual depictions of black artists, scientists, politicians, philosophers, and everyday people?

With this song, have the grown-ups form two lines and stand facing each other. If they extend their arms and hold each other's hands, they'll form a tunnel for the kids to dance through. For extra excitement, if the music suddenly stops, the tunnel can drop down, capturing any dancers within reach. ✳

LISTEN . . .

Lead Belly Sings for Children and *Lead Belly: The Smithsonian Folkways Collection,* both by Lead Belly

12-String Guitar as Played by Lead Belly by Pete Seeger

Lead Belly, Baby! by Dan Zanes and Friends

READ . . .

Roots, Radicals, and Rockers: How Skiffle Changed the World by Billy Bragg

Lead Belly: A Life in Pictures by Tiny Robinson, John Reynolds, and Tyehimba Jess, editors

Lead Belly: Poems by Tyehimba Jess

With Vocal Quartet Energy

2 May be right, may be wrong,
   I know you're going to miss me when I'm gone.

3 Jesus died to save our sins,
   Glory to God, I'm going to see Him again.

4 Train left Memphis at half past nine,
   Pulled into Little Rock at 8:55.

Huddie Ledbetter, Alan Lomax.
Folkways Music Publishers, Inc. (BMI).
From *Lead Belly, Baby!* by Dan Zanes and Friends.

With Seeds and Soul

Oh, the farm-er comes to town with his wa-gon brok-en down, The farm-er is the one who feeds them all. If you'll on-ly look and see, I think you will a-gree that the farm-er is the one who feeds them all._____ The

Chorus:

farm-er is the one, the farm-er is the one.

Lives on cred-it 'til the fall, Ev-ery wo-man, child, and man, I think will un-der-stand, That the farm-er is the one who feeds them all.

Public Domain, arranged by Dan Zanes. Published by Sister Barbara Music (ASCAP).
From *Little Nut Tree* by Dan Zanes and Friends.

THE FARMER IS THE ONE

2 Well, the lawyer stands around
While the butcher cuts a pound,
He forgets that it's the farmer feeds 'em all.
And the preacher and the cook
Go a-strollin' by the brook,
They forget that it's the farmer feeds 'em all.

The farmer is the one, the farmer is the one.
Lives on credit 'til the fall,
With the interest rate so high
It's a wonder he don't die,
And the middleman's the one who gets it all.

3 When the banker says he's broke
And the merchant's up in smoke,
They forget that it's the farmer feeds 'em all.
If he'd only take a rest,
He could put 'em to the test,
'Cause the farmer is the one who feeds 'em all.

The farmer is the one, the farmer is the one.
Lives on credit 'til the fall,
His condition it's a sin
'Cause his pants are getting thin,
We forgot that he's the one who feeds us all.

Here's a song from the 1890s populist movement in America. It first appeared in the Farmers' Alliance songbook (at sixty cents a copy!) with the title "The Farmer Is the Man."

Farmers were working together to achieve some political clout as they faced difficulties in the market. Crops were failing, prices were falling, credit was difficult to obtain, and farms lacked support and stability. But the farmers had collective energy and vision . . . and they had songs! Author Nathan Schneider, comparing this with current sentiments, called it "a populism of hope, not a populism of fear."

It's worth noting that Pete Seeger freely changed lyrics to suit the needs of the day. "The Farmer Is the Man" became "The Farmer Is the One" to include the women working the land. In this way Pete ensured that the songs didn't become irrelevant, dusty relics sitting on the back shelves of our minds.

If you feel that some of the songs in this book need updating, go for it. Pete never seemed to lose the original spirit of the tunes, and I hope that along the way we don't either. ✱

LISTEN . . .
"The Farmer Is the Man That Feeds Them All"
by Fiddlin' John Carson (first recorded version)

American Industrial Ballads
by Pete Seeger

READ . . .
Carry It On: The Story of America's Working People in Song and Picture by Pete Seeger and Bob Reiser

Folk Song USA by John and Alan Lomax

YES! magazine

SMILE, SMILE, SMILE

Mid-Tempo Bounce

Eve-ry time that I think of_____ you, I
Acting out stories and_____ hug-ging your friends,_____

smile for a while.
Smile for a while.

That's the one thing you al-ways do, You al-ways
Know what I'll do when I see you again I'm going to

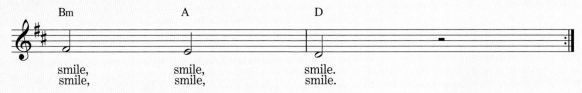

smile, smile, smile.
smile, smile, smile.

Chorus:

Like rip-ples_ in a pond_____ Or run-ners that pass the ba-ton,_____

The good fee-lings will go on for mile af-ter mile____ And your

big heart cir-cles the world every time____ that you smile.

Written by Dan Zanes. Published by Sister Barbara Music (ASCAP).
From *Night Time!* by Dan Zanes and Friends.

3 Doing those voices and telling your jokes,
Smile for a while.
The crazy hairdos and the thrift shop coats,
They make me smile, smile, smile.

4 Every time you break into a Broadway song,
Smile for a while.
Everyone around you starts singing along,
We smile, smile, smile.

5 Well you know I love you
And I'm glad you're my friend,
Smile for a while.
You know what I'll do when I see you again,
Smile, smile, smile,
Smile, smile, smile.

This might be a good song to sing for grandmothers and grandfathers. Not all grandparents are the same, of course, but if we can make a few generalizations it might be fair to say that they are the best dancers; they know a lot of old jokes; sometimes they eat odd food, but for the most part, they are good cooks; they have some secret knowledge when it comes to music; they can be pretty funny without meaning to be; they love naps; they can be quite patient when others get all worked up; they know some strange stories; they like to make time to hang out; sometimes they're cranky; and they appreciate how much they are loved.

This is a good song for social singalongs. People just need to learn two lines "Smile for a while" and "Smile, smile, smile." If the singing is strong, the group could learn the last line ". . . and your big heart circles the world every time that you smile," and belt it out at the end of each chorus.

Let me take this opportunity to remind you that you might not have the right song for every occasion. There may be times when you'll need something new. Feel free to grab an old melody and add new words. Or write a whole song. I encourage you to jump right in—you can do this! ✳

READ . . .
Sammy Cahn's Rhyming Dictionary by Sammy Cahn

LISTEN . . .
Shake Sugaree: Taj Mahal Sings and Plays for Children by Taj Mahal

My Name Is Buddy by Ry Cooder

Alerta Sings and Songs for the Playground (Canciones Para el Recreo) by Suni Paz

OLD JOE CLARK

"Songs which were used to being thrown around, played with, joked with . . . no wonder such songs could make us feel at home with ourselves and with each other: they were seasoned travelers. Songs like these could easily take on the color and spirit of any situation."

—Ruth Crawford Seeger,
American Folk Songs for Children

T hese verses are just a start . . . you can easily find dozens more. And don't forget to make up some of your own!

The intersection of early-childhood education and southern mountain or old-time music is a beautiful place. The roots are deep but the songs themselves, when grasped and sung by children, are alive and up-to-date. The old foolishness finds new expression in the musical classroom or home.

When asking the children to dance, the movement for this song in its simplest form can be the motion of turning around and around, as the lyrics suggest. The tempo can get faster or slower, the volume can rise and fall. Dizzy dancers can collapse on the ground, and the song can fall with them until a rousing cry of, "Now get back up, Old Joe Clark!" gets the party back in high gear. These are only a few suggestions. Any fun-loving educator or caregiver can cook up many more on the spot.

I went to my first bluegrass festival in Summersville, West Virginia, somewhere around 1988. My brother-in-law at the time, Barry Wine (cousin of the old-time fiddler Melvin Wine!), and I loaded up his friend Mike's RV with guitars and enough food for the weekend and hit the scene. It was a pivotal experience for me. The music onstage seemed no more important than the music in the parking lot. The star system that I was so used to in rock and roll was practically nonexistent. It was community and it was all-ages. It was bluegrass and it was old-time. It was pretty clear to me that if talk turned to politics, we might not find much common ground, but what a blessing to find our shared humanity in the sound of banjo, mandolin, guitar, bass, and fiddle. By the end of the weekend I'd made the decision that if I couldn't play music that invited and united, I would pack it in and become a gardener . . . round and round, Old Joe Clark! ✱

LISTEN . . .
Legends of Old-Time Music: Fifty Years of County Records
by various artists

Bill Monroe and His Bluegrass Boys . . . it's hard to go wrong with the "Father of Bluegrass"—try any of them.

East Virginia Blues: The Secret History of Rock & Roll
by various artists

READ . . .
Rural Roots of Bluegrass: Songs, Stories & History by Wayne Erbsen

African Banjo Echoes in Appalachia: A Study of Folk Traditions by Cecelia Conway

WATCH . . .
High Lonesome: The Story of Bluegrass Music
directed by Rachel Liebling

With a Fiddle Tune Pace

Old Joe Clark he had a house Eight - een stor - ies high.

Ev - ery sto - ry in that house Was filled with chick - en pie.

Chorus:

'Round and 'round, Old Joe Clark, 'Round and 'round, I say.

'Round and 'round, Old Joe Clark, I ain't got long to stay.

2 I went down to Old Joe's house,
He invited me to supper.
I stumped my toe on the table leg
And stuck my nose in the butter.

3 Roll around, Old Joe Clark,
Sail away and gone.
Roll around, Old Joe Clark,
With your golden slippers on.

4 I went down to Old Joe's house,
Never been there before.
He slept on a feather bed,
I slept on the floor.

5 Old Joe Clark, he had a cow,
She was muley born.
Take a jaybird a week and a half
To fly from horn to horn.

6 Old Joe Clark had a mule,
His name was Morgan Brown.
And every tooth in that mule's head
Was sixteen inches around.

7 When I was a little kid
I used to play in ashes.
Now you see, I'm all grown up,
Wearing Dad's moustaches.

Traditional, arranged by Dan Zanes. Published by Sister Barbara Music (ASCAP).
From *House Party* by Dan Zanes and Friends.

HOW DO YOU DO?

With Music Hall Timing

You've heard of the late-est craze that's out, A new style of greet-ing with-out a doubt. The

old style of greet-ing was "How do you do?" But the John-nies have gone in for a style quite new.

When a John-nie meets a John-nie in the street, He rai-ses his hat in a style so neat, Shakes

hands in the us-u-al or-tho-dox way, Then one to the o-ther will be sure to say...

Chorus:

How do you doo-dle-oo-dle oo-dle-oo-dle-oo? How do you doo-dle-oo-dle-oo-dle-oo-dle oo?

Aw-fully pleased for to meet, meet you, How do you doo-dle-oo-dle-oo-dle-oo-dle-oo?

Public Domain, arranged by Dan Zanes. Published by Sister Barbara Music (ASCAP).
From House Party by Dan Zanes and Friends.

2 Everybody's got it, both the young and
   the old,
The high and the low, the meek and the bold.
There's a policeman out on the street,
That's the style of greeting when a friend
   he'll meet.
Then there's a lassie when she meets a pal,
She'll say, "Ah, begorrah, now you're looking
   mighty well."
Shakes hands in the usual orthodox way,
Then one to the other will be sure to say . . .

During their heyday in the late 1800s, English music halls had it all. Food! Drink! Comedy! Trampoline acts! Fire-eaters! Talking dogs! Stilt walkers! Shadow puppets! Flea circuses! Ventriloquists! And many, many fine singers with humorous and sentimental songs such as "How Do You Do?" It's been said that a music hall song had to be so catchy that the audience would be singing along *by the end of the first public performance!*

   English rock bands like the Beatles and the Kinks were clearly influenced by music hall songs. Probably Queen, too. Certainly Herman's Hermits were: they had a hit with the music hall number, "I'm Henry the VIII, I Am." The Hermits didn't even bother with the verses—they sang the chorus four times and called it a day—and the song went to No. 1 on the charts! Maybe your family band will suddenly realize that comical portraits of everyday life with memorable singalong refrains are a nice way to go. When you have your first gig, don't forget to invite some trick cyclists.✳

LISTEN . . .
Round the Town: Following Grandfather's Footsteps by various artists. **This four-CD set features vintage music hall memories, including "How Do You Do?"**

Widdecombe Fair by David Jones and Bill Shute. **David is one of the world's finest practitioners of English music hall, but this collection is a different bag: a record of classic folk music he made for young people in the early 1980s.**

READ . . .
British Music Hall: An Illustrated History by Richard Anthony Baker

Sixty Years of British Music Hall: Popular Music, Comic Songs, Songbook by John M. Garrett

BY AND BY
SONGS OF LOVE & COMMUNITY

THE PARTY

ATTITUDES AND INVITATIONS

Getting you ready to hit the stage isn't really the goal of this book, but I've performed in thrift shop basements and Carnegie Hall (and many points in between) and learned a couple of things that I can pass along.

Shows are most enjoyable when I really *know* the songs. The lyrics are in my brain, my fingers can find the right chord at the right time, and I have a good sense of the historical background. It's possible to go into situations half-baked, winging it here and there, but that can be unsatisfying for the audience. People know when we're *inside* the material. That's my first suggestion: do your homework.

I've gone into performances thinking there would be five hundred people in attendance but there were only fifty. Other times, only my mother came out. In all situations, I have to remember that I'm there to give. If I'm prepared and I show up with a generous spirit, nothing can go wrong. I try to share the music with heart and sincerity knowing that that's the opportunity God offered that day. So, there's my second suggestion: show up to give.

Make it a point to think along racial lines to see if everyone has been invited to the party. When a mixed group plays for a white audience in a multicultural town or neighborhood, there are probably some missed opportunities. The strongest organizations I've worked with have been multiracial. If there are solid relationships across communities, it's easier to spread the word effectively. Flyers and social media alone don't usually work well without real relationships to help generate enthusiasm for a show.

The third and final point here has to do with accessibility and inclusion. Wheelchair ramps weren't always a consideration, but fortunately today they're somewhat standard. Venue conditions that are comfortable for people on the autism spectrum and for those with sensory differences are not the norm yet, but that's changing too. There are a variety of names for performances that take these conditions into account. "Sensory-friendly" and "relaxed" are the most common.

One of the more important aspects of a sensory-friendly performance, in addition to sound and light modifications, is invitational language indicating a welcoming and supportive environment for those with autism and other neurodevelopmental disabilities. The door is already open to many of us and sensory-friendly is a way of opening it a little wider so that more people feel welcomed. Information about making a show sensory-friendly can be found online. The Kennedy Center/VSA in Washington, DC, has a very comprehensive guide on their website.

Music making is a joyous experience, something to be celebrated and shared. It's something that we can do individually and, in its ultimate form, it's something we do *with* each other and *for* each other. There's nothing more uplifting than belting out some songs knowing that as many people as possible were invited to the party.

THE WELCOME TABLE

This song has been known by several titles, including "I'm Going to Sit at the Welcome Table" and "River Jordan," but the message of justice and inclusion is the same in all of them. During the Civil Rights movement in the United States, the words were updated to reflect the challenges of the day—voter registration and segregation, in particular—as heard in the version by Hollis Watkins.

Although we talk about the flexible nature of folk songs, it's important for me to consider where to draw the line. There are songs that just aren't mine to mess with, and one like this so strongly connected to the African American story would be in that category. I was once asked to change the words to "The Welcome Table" for a children's TV show and sing "I'm going to play with all of my toys." I thank my friend Toshi Reagon for making it very clear to me that this isn't my song to change—especially not in that way! It's important to recognize that this song, and many others like it, holds very deep meaning to many people and speaks to struggles that are real to this day.

"The Welcome Table" has a message that most anyone can support—who wouldn't want to live where all are accepted and welcomed? And me, as a white guy who's *always* been at the welcome table . . . how do I sing this one? It took me a while, but the answer is that I sing it with a desire to sit at the table that's truely set for one and all. We don't have that table now, but we will someday. And what a feast we'll have. ✳

LISTEN . . .

Sing for Freedom: The Story of the Civil Rights Movement through Its Songs and *Voices of the Civil Rights Movement: Black American Freedom Songs 1960–1966,* both by various artists

"The Welcome Table" by Dan Zanes and Friends feat. The Blind Boys of Alabama

"I'm Going to Walk and Talk with Jesus" by Clara Ward & The Ward Singers

"I'm Going to Walk and Talk with Jesus" by Shirley Caesar

"The River of Jordan" by The Carter Family

READ . . .

Dismantling Racism by Joseph R. Barndt

With Conviction and Feel

2 I'm going to feast on milk and honey . . .

3 I'm going to break bread with my neighbor . . .

4 I'm going to tell God how you treat me . . .

5 I'm going to view that holy city . . .

6 I'm going to sing and never get tired . . .

7 I'm going to be a registered voter . . .

8 I'm going to sit at the Woolworth counter . . .

9 I'm going to walk and talk with Jesus . . .

Traditional, arranged by Dan Zanes. Published by Sister Barbara Music (ASCAP).
From *Catch That Train* by Dan Zanes and Friends.

LORD LOVEL

With Storytelling Heart

Lord Lov-el,___ he stood at his cas-tle gate,

Comb-ing his milk-white steed, When a-

long came La-dy Nan-cy Bell,

Wish-ing___ her lov-er good speed, speed, speed,

Wish-ing___ her lov-er___ good speed.

2 "Oh where are you going, Lord Lovel?"
she said,
"Oh where are you going?" said she.
"I'm going, my dear Lady Nancy Bell,
Strange countries for to see, see, see,
Strange countries for to see."

3 "When will you be back, Lord Lovel?"
she said,
"When will you be back?" said she.
"In a year or two or three at the most,
I'll return to my Lady Nancy-cee, cee,
I'll return to my Lady Nancy."

4 He had not been gone but a year and a
day,
Strange countries for to see,
When languishing thoughts came into
his mind,
Lady Nancy Bell he would see.

5 He rode and he rode on his milk-white
steed,
Till he reached fair London Town.
There he heard St. Varney's bell
And the people all mourning around.

6 "Is anyone dead?" Lord Lovel he said,
"Is anyone dead?" said he.
"A lady is dead," the people all said,
"And they called her Lady Nancy."

BY AND BY

Traditional, arranged by Dan Zanes. Published by Sister Barbara Music (ASCAP).
From *Parades and Panoramas: 25 Songs Collected by Carl Sandburg for The American Songbag* by Dan Zanes and Friends.

7 He ordered the grave to be opened forthwith,
The shroud to be folded down.
Then he kissed her clay-cold lips
Till the tears came trickling down.

8 Lady Nancy she died as it might be today,
Lord Lovel he died tomorrow.
Lady Nancy she died of pure, pure grief,
Lord Lovel he died of sorrow.

9 Lady Nancy was laid
in St. Clement's churchyard,
Lord Lovel buried close by her.
Out of her bosom there grew a red rose,
And out of his backbone a briar.

10 They grew and they grew
on the old church tower,
Till they couldn't grow up any higher.
There they tied in a true lover's knot,
For all true lovers to admire.

READ . . .

The English and Scottish Popular Ballads, Vols. 1–10
collected by Francis James Child

Electric Eden: Unearthing Britain's Visionary Music
by Rob Young

Dazzling Stranger: Bert Jansch and the British Folk and Blues Revival by Colin Harper

LISTEN . . .

Topic Records: The Real Sound of Folk Music by various artists

The Fox Jumps over the Parson's Gate by Peter Bellamy

So Cheerfully Round by The Young Tradition

The Voice of the People, Vols. 1–20. This is a beautiful collection of English music on Topic Records organized by theme. Anglophiles, run, don't walk, to this collection!

Hundreds of years! Very few things that aren't plastic or stone can last that long, but this song has been around since the Middle Ages. A remarkable achievement—will we be singing "Octopus's Garden" in 2418?

In this song, Lord Lovel tells his true love, Lady Nancy Bell, that he's going away for a few years to see strange countries. After a year (and a day), he feels the need to get back to Lady Nancy, but upon his return he finds that she's died. She died of grief, and he is so overcome with sorrow that he dies too. In the end, a rose and a briar grow from their graves and intertwine.

The concept of the "signature song" is a heavy one. The way it works is that everyone has a tune that they can be counted on to sing when the situation arises. It's generally the same song, regardless of the gathering. I was at a wild party a few years back and just when I thought it couldn't get any more unhinged, everyone started saying, "Wait, wait, it's time for Dorothy! Aunt Dorothy's song!" The room suddenly became very quiet and Dorothy stood up and sang an acapella version of "Barbara Allen." That's a long song, too, but the room was quiet and focused, as if they were hearing it for the first time. What I found out later was that "Barbara Allen" was Aunt Dorothy's signature song and therefore a part of every musical gathering. My signature song is "Lord Lovel." What's yours?

This song is also what's known as a "Child Ballad." In the late 1800s, Boston scholar Francis James Child began gathering and categorizing folk ballads. The result was ten volumes of deep research, which became the standard for many, many years. "Lord Lovel" is Child Ballad 75. I think it might be time for a version in which Lord Lovel stays home and Lady Nancy goes to see some strange countries for a change! ✱

TRAIN IS A-COMING

Let's contemplate train songs for a minute. "I'm Going Home on the Morning Train." "The Gospel Train Is Coming." "This Train is Bound for Glory." "Soul Train." "Take the A Train." "Ride This Train." "Jim Crow Train." "Last Train to Expo '67." "Train Kept a Rollin'." "Mystery Train." "Peace Train." "Love Train." "Freedom Train." "Hear My Train A-Comin'." "Freight Train." "Midnight Train to Georgia." "Stop That Train." "Party Train." "Don't Miss That Train." "Zion Train." "Black Train Blues." "Last Train." "Blue Train." "Go Go Train." "Train to Skaville." "Everybody Loves a Train." "Don't Stop This Train." "Night Train to Moscow." "Catch That Train and Ride." The list goes on and on, like a train.

This train song began its life as an African American spiritual and, over the years, has become one of the classic songs used by early-childhood educators. Its depth, simplicity, and sense of mystery, possibility, and urgency make it a natural song for almost any occasion. Many times, this song has been adapted to make verses with each child's name, e.g., "Rosetta is conductor, oh yeah . . ." and so on. ✱

LISTEN . . .

Spirituals by Marian Anderson

Gospels, Spirituals & Hymns and *In My Home Over There*, both by Mahalia Jackson

Classic Railroad Songs from Smithsonian Folkways by various artists

READ . . .

John Henry by Julius Lester and Jerry Pinkney

All Night, All Day: A Child's First Book of African-American Spirituals by Ashley Bryan

ELLA JENKINS

The First Lady of Children's Music! That's Ella Jenkins (1924 –).

I don't recall my first exposure to her but she was certainly there from the beginning. There's no doubt that before I was collecting memories, I was hearing the music of Ella Jenkins.

Ella Jenkins was multicultural before there was such a word in the mainstream conversation. She led by example and made it wildly attractive. Songs from near and far, old and new, serious and funny, always simple enough to grab ahold of and quite often deep enough to want to carry through life.

Ella's first record, released in 1957, set the tone for much of her career. *Call and Response: Rhythmic Group Singing* featured songs from West Africa that she performed with a group of young people. For over fifty years and almost fifty records, she has connected children to music and culture in a way unsurpassed in American musical history.

She sang of Puerto Rico and Switzerland, frogs and koalas, holidays and rainy days, neighborhoods and outer space, libraries and freedom trains. Ella Jenkins introduced the concept of unions to children in a way that a three-year-old could understand!

From the 1950s through the early twenty-first century, as society became increasingly fragmented and mechanized, she grounded young people in music and found ways to let them know that music was our common language.

As we continually try to figure out how to raise our children to be global citizens, engaged, curious, and excited, it's important to remember that Ella Jenkins has been showing us the way all along.

Slowly and Thoughtfully

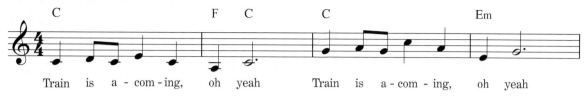

Train is a - com - ing, oh yeah   Train is a - com - ing, oh yeah

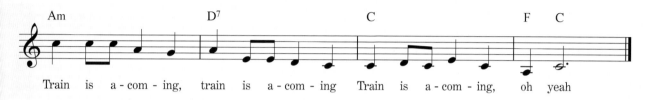

Train is a - com - ing, train is a - com - ing   Train is a - com - ing, oh yeah

2 Better get your ticket, oh yeah . . .

3 There's room for many more, oh yeah . . .

4 Change is a-coming, oh yeah . . .

Traditional, arranged by Dan Zanes & Elizabeth Mitchell. Published by Sister Barbara Music (ASCAP) and Last Affair Music (BMI).
***From Parades and Panoramas: 25 Songs Collected by Carl Sandburg for The American Songbag** by Dan Zanes and Friends.*

DIU DIU DENG

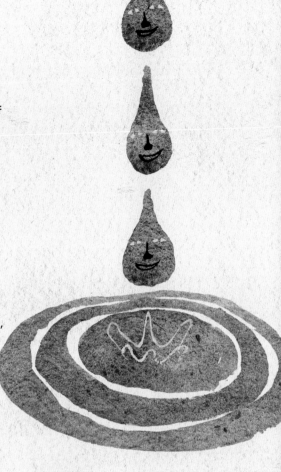

Elena Moon Park is back with another wild folk song, this one from Taiwan.

"I learned this from my friend Ya Yun. 'Diu Diu Deng' is about a train chugging through a tunnel as droplets of water fall from the ceiling onto the tops of the moving cars. The droplets make a sound, *Diu Diu*, like the sound of a falling coin landing on the floor. This melody is believed to have come into existence around the beginning of nineteenth century, when Chinese immigrant Wu Sha led 1,000 settlers from China's Fujian and Guangdong provinces to Yilan County in Taiwan.

"While it is most fun to shout along to the 'Diu! Diu!' found in the middle of the rhyme, I also encourage listeners to try and learn the playful Taiwanese lyrics. The rhymes of 'gia dao ito-ama-ito' and 'Dang a ito ama ito/Diu ah ito' are enjoyable both sung and spoken, whether you know the Taiwanese language or not.

"This song is often performed by choirs in Mandarin, Taiwanese, and other languages, oftentimes in a round, and emulating the sounds of a train. In my version, we combine the sound of the Chinese pipa with the banjo and speed up the tempo like the acceleration of a train!" ✳

READ . . .

The Rough Guide to World Music: Europe, Asia & Pacific by Jon Lusk, editor

Live at the Forbidden City: Musical Encounters in China and Taiwan by Dennis Rea

LISTEN . . .

Rabbit Days and Dumplings by Elena Moon Park and Friends

Also check out Ara Kimbo, an indigenous Taiwanese singer known as "The Father of Taiwanese Folk Songs," and Chen Ming-Chang, an important Taiwanese artist who came out of the campus folk song movement and has had a decades-long career.

A search for Taiwanese campus folk song generally leads to many melodic musical riches from this important movement in which Taiwanese youth advocated for their own cultural expressions. This break from Western cultural dominance caught fire in the 1970s and 1980s.

With a Slow (or Fast!) Train Rhythm

Huei chia gia dao it - o am-a it-o diu A-yo bong kahng lai Bong kahng et-su it-o

diu diu Dang a it-o a-ma it-o Diu a it-o di lo lai

Bong kahng et-su it-o diu diu Dang a it-o a-ma it-o Diu a it-o

di lo lai_____

Atrain is chug-chug-ging

in - to a tunnel Where the water drips down Makes a sound like a "Diu Diu" Sound like a

coin When it's flipped up and drops to the floor.

Makes a sound__ like a "Diu Diu" Sound__ like a

coin__ When it's flipped up and drops to the floor_____

Traditional, arranged by Elena Moon Park. Published by Moonpark Music (ASCAP).
From *Rabbit Days and Dumplings* by Elena Moon Park and Friends.

COUNTRY LIFE

I flipped when I first heard The Watersons sing this song on their *For Pence and Spicy Ale* record. I looked for anything I could find by this group, known in their heyday as the "Folk Beatles." They were English hipsters with tight pants, long hair, turtlenecks, and attitude, but also hipsters who were serious about their heritage. This was my introduction to the importance of cultural identity. Here was a group of cool young people looking for agricultural songs, hunting songs, and historical narratives from their region: East Yorkshire in the north of England. They said that they "picked up the threads of a tradition" and made sure to acknowledge those who came before them. The Watersons made me want to stop climbing all over other people's family trees and take a look at my own.

The word "laylum" is somewhat obscure, but in this song seems to mean either a piece of farmland or a chorus that birds might sing. (Eliza Carthy, daughter of Watersons member Martin Carthy, says this is what The Watersons meant.) ✳

LISTEN . . .

Early Days by The Watersons

Essential by Martin Carthy

Come Write Me Down: Early Recordings of the Copper Family of Rottingdean by Copper Family

READ . . .

Singing from the Floor: A History of British Folk Clubs by J. P. Bean

With Morning Sun Gusto

Chorus:

I like to rise when the sun she rise-es, ear-ly in the morn-ing I like to hear them small birds sing-ing Merr-i-ly up-on their lay-lums. And hurr-ah for the life of a coun-try kid And to ram-ble in the new mowed hay. In the spring we sow in the har-vest mow, That's how the sea-sons around they go. But of all the times to choose I may, I'd be ram-bling through the new mowed hay.

2. In winter when the sky is gray
We hedge and ditch our times away.
But in summer when the sun shines gay,
We go ramblin' through the new mowed hay.

Traditional, arranged by Dan Zanes. Published by Sister Barbara Music (ASCAP).
From *Catch That Train* by Dan Zanes and Friends.

SO GLAD I'M HERE

"So Glad I'm Here" comes from the African American gospel tradition, and the lyrics generally say, "So glad I'm here in Jesus' name." There are a few versions of the song; I've included the simpler one, which was inspired by Bessie Jones of the Georgia Sea Island Singers. The way she approaches it is straightforward, strong, and soulful: tambourine, hand claps, and voices taking the message right to the heart. The folk music of the Georgia Sea Islands is generally heavy on vocals and percussion, and the recordings that exist from that region are easily some of the most powerful ever created in America.

Now let's shift for a minute, go deep, and appreciate some of the many female African American gospel singers who have practiced their artistry at the highest levels imaginable: Dorothy Love Coates, Shirley Caesar, Mahalia Jackson, The Caravans, Rosetta Tharpe, Dorothy Norwood, Albertina Walker, Marie Knight, Mavis Staples, Clara Ward, the Davis Sisters, Bessie Griffin, Cassietta George, Madame Edna Gallmon Cooke, Marion Williams, Sallie Martin, Willie Mae Ford Smith . . . and these are just the ones I know and love. We're only scratching the surface here, people!

It would be impossible to understand popular music in twentieth-century America without understanding black gospel music to some degree. Changes in technology may have negatively altered the financial situation for recording artists, but they've also made it easy for the curious public to find and hear a broad range of recorded music from the last century. Don't hold back—yesterday, today, and tomorrow are all in these songs. ✳

READ . . .

African American Heritage Hymnal by Rev. Dr. Delores Carpenter, general editor

The Gospel Sound: Good News and Bad Times by Anthony Heilbut

How Sweet the Sound: The Golden Age of Gospel by Horace Clarence Boyer

We'll Understand It Better By and By: Pioneering African American Gospel Composers by Dr. Bernice Johnson Reagon

LISTEN . . .

So Glad I'm Here and *Step It Up!*, both by Bessie Jones

Down Home by the Jackson Southernaires

Get on Board by Dorothy Love Coates and The Original Gospel Harmonettes

The Gospel Sound

The Best of Nashboro Gospel

Wade in the Water: African American Sacred Music Traditions, Vols. I–IV

Precious Lord: Recordings of the Great Gospel Songs of Thomas A. Dorsey, all by various artists

Joyfully

I'm so___ glad I'm here, I'm so___ glad I'm here, I'm

so___ glad I'm here, here to-day.___ I'm so___ glad I'm here, I'm

so___ glad I'm here, I'm so___ glad I'm here, here to-day.

2 I'm going to sing while I'm here . . .

3 Love brought me here . . .

4 Joy brought me here . . .

5 I'm going to dance while I'm here . . .

Bessie Jones, Alan Lomax. Ludlow Music, Inc. (BMI).
From *Turn Turn Turn* by Dan Zanes and Elizabeth Mitchell
with You Are My Flower.

PANAMA MWEN TOMBÉ

In this song, the president of Haiti in the late 1800s, Louis Mondestin Florvil Hyppolite, is getting ready to take a trip to La Vallée. As he is mounting his horse, *on a perfectly still day*, his Panama hat blows off. A bad omen, as there is no wind! He asks someone to pick it up for him and continues with his plans, ignoring this sign that he should cancel the trip. Along the way, he has a heart attack and dies.

This is an extremely popular song in Haiti and has been for generations. I've never met a Haitian over the age of thirty who wouldn't sing along when "Panama Mwen Tombé" was played. Everyone knows it! There are rustic folk *twoubadou* versions, high-energy *konpa* versions, and everything in between. This is an all-purpose social song, and my hope is that if you're not already familiar with Haitian music, food, painting, sculpture, literature, language, history, folklore, philosophy, and, above all, people, this song will inspire you to make it happen.

My life was forever changed when I began to learn about Haiti and the Haitian people. I thank my friends, neighbors, and my beautiful Haitian wife, Claudia, and her family (now *our* family) for taking the time to help me understand the culture—and for always letting me practice my Kreyol! ✱

READ . . .

A Day for the Hunter, a Day for the Prey: Popular Music and Power in Haiti by Gage Averill

Konpa Encyclopedia by Professor Jean Claude Vivens

Haiti Uncovered: A Regional Adventure into the Art of Haitian Cuisine by Nadege Fleurimond

Creole Without Fuss and Tears by Deslande Rincher

Krik? Krak! by Edwidge Danticat

LISTEN . . .

I'm going to do it a little differently here and just give a list of artists. Almost everything they've released is special in some way. Dig in and enjoy. *Bon Bagay!*: Coupé Cloué, Trio Select, Webert Sicot, Orchestre Tropicana d'Haiti, Leon Dimanche, Fedia Laguerre, Skah-Shah, Shleu-Shleu, Ti Manno, Scorpio Universel, Les Loups Noir, Rodrigue Milien, Tabou Combo, Magnum Band, Bossa Combo, Étoile du Soir, Joe Jack, DP Express, Les Fantaisistes De Carrefour, Zekle, Caribbean Sextet, Ibo Combo, Super Soline, Nemours Jean-Baptiste, Super Jazz Des Jeunes, Les Gypsies, Les Dificiles, Orchestre Septentrional, Issa El Saieh . . . and this is just the beginning. There is so much to the music and culture of Haiti. I could listen to this music all day. Come to think of it, that's exactly what I do!

With Festive Energy

Mwen so-ti la-vil Jac-mel, Mwen pral-e La-vall e. En arr-i-vanm ka-fou Be-né,

1. Pa-na-ma mwen tom-bé!

2. Pa-na-ma mwen tom-bé!

Chorus: Pa-na-ma mwen tom-bé,

Pa-na-ma mwen tom-bé, Pa-na-ma mwen tom-bé, Sa-ki-di-yé, Ran-man se li pou mwen.

Pa-na-ma mwen tom-bé, Pa-na-ma mwen tom-bé,

Pa-na-ma mwen tom-bé, Sa-ki-di-yé, Ran-man-se li pou mwen.

LOOSE TRANSLATION:

I left the city of Jacmel,

I went to La Vallée.

When I got to the intersection at Bainet,

My hat fell off!

My hat fell off!

My hat fell off,

My hat fell off,

My hat fell off,

Whoever is behind me,

Please pick it up for me.

Traditional, arranged by Dan Zanes. Published by Sister Barbara Music (ASCAP).
From *It's A Bam Bam Diddly!* by Father Goose.

105

CATCH THAT TRAIN

Three chords over and over (and over and over) again with a slogan perched on top. That's it. I say this to encourage songwriting. Everyone can agree that it's not the complexity of a song that makes it successful any more than it's the number of bones in the skeletal system that makes an animal interesting to watch. One of my favorite styles of music is 1960s Jamaican rocksteady. The groups from that era turned three chords and a slogan into high art again and again.

When I wrote this, I was thinking about the trains that run from New York City up the Hudson River and how train travel is so much more social than plane travel. No seatbelts! Wider aisles! Get up, walk around, visit people in the other cars, sing, eat lunch, read, and, of course, write songs.

One great party idea for a song like this is to have people stand up and put their hands on someone's shoulders so they're facing the back of that person's head. The participants connect to each other until there are . . . trains! It's always fun, whether there are young people or not. Any look at a conga line during a bar mitzvah or bat mitzvah will tell you that this is something we humans just like to do for a good time. ✳

LISTEN . . .
Beverley's Records: The Collection, Duke Reid's Treasure Chest, and *Let's Do Rocksteady: The Story of Rocksteady 1966–68,* all by various artists

Version Galore by U-Roy

READ . . .
Stir It Up: Reggae Cover Art by Chris Morrow

People Funny Boy: The Genius of Lee "Scratch" Perry by David Katz

SPOONS AND BONES

They're really two very different instruments, so why group spoons and bones together? Because this humble book isn't a thousand pages long and I'm trying to jam as much information as possible between the covers, that's why! Plus, both are held in the hands and can easily fit in a shirt pocket.

Basic spoon playing can be learned in the time it takes to clear the dinner dishes and get dessert ready—it doesn't take much practice to feel a sense of accomplishment, and there's a rich history to examine: Canada, Britain, Russia, Greece, and Turkey all have strong spoon-playing traditions.

The basic idea with spoons is to hold two of them in one hand so the curved backs face each other with a small amount of space between them. When the spoons are tapped against a thigh or another hand (or the skull!), a metallic sound is produced. Depending on the size of the hand, soup spoons or regular teaspoons will work.

Bones (or "clappers" or "knicky-knackers") are another thing altogether. Early forms of the instrument date back to 2000 BC, usually made of cattle ribs. In her paper "Bones: Ancient to Modern," Sue E. Barber writes that they were likely used for worship as well as amusement in, among other places, Egypt and ancient Rome. Fast forward to the 1800s and the bones were a part of rural black musical ensembles in the United States. We can find the rural roots of bones playing in the modern performances of Dom Flemons the American Songster, his former group the Carolina Chocolate Drops, and Hubby Jenkins.

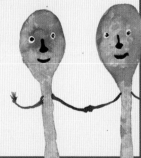

With Summer Enthusiasm

Ev-ery-bo-dy's talk-ing a-bout a day up at the lake, So let's

get our bags and gui-tars and all the food that we can take._____ I'll

meet you on the cor-ner when the sun de-cides to break._____ So

Chorus:

catch that___ train,_____ Come on out___ and catch it,

catch that___ train,_____

2. I don't mind the station, I don't mind going
   underground.
   I kind of like the symphony of a thousand
   different sounds.
   In another twenty minutes we'll all be country
   bound.

3. We'll look out of the window and watch the
   world go flying past,
   Every river, town, and village as they come
   and go so fast.
   We'll fill the day with memories, I know
   they're going to last.

4. It's a topsy-turvy world that we're all living in
   today.
   Let's take a trip before the summer sun has
   gone astray.
   When we ride, we ride together and so I say:

Written by Dan Zanes. Published by Sister Barbara Music (ASCAP).
From *Catch That Train* by Dan Zanes and Friends.

EL BOTELLÓN

Mid-Tempo Social Gusto

Solo: Ay por a - quí pas - ó mi sue - gra

Chorus: Con el bo - te - llón,___ Con el bo - te - llón.

Solo: Ay mi sue - gra mi sue - gra

Chorus: Con el bo - te - llón,_____ Con el bo - te - llón.

Solo: Ay vend - ien - do re - poll - o

Chorus: Con el bo - te - llón,_____ Con el bo - te - llón.

Solo: Ay re - poll - o re - poll - o

Chorus: Con el bo - te - llón,_____ Con el bo - te - llón.

Continue call and response
for more verses...

Traditional, arranged by Dan Zanes. Published by Sister Barbara Music (ASCAP).
From *¡Nueva York!* by Dan Zanes and Friends.

Oh my mother-in-law passed through here
Oh my mother-in-law
Oh selling cabbage
Oh cabbage, cabbage

2
¿Cómo lo vende?
Ay va por el callejón
Ay ¿a cómo lo vende?
Ay se va con el botellón
How do you sell it?
Oh down the alley
Oh how do you sell it?
Oh with the bottle

3
Additional lyrics by La Bruja:
Mi linda suegra con piel de canela,
Buscando agua para cocinar su miel de abeja.
Curandera, con remedios que le enseñó la
   abuela.
My good mother-in-law with her cinnamon
   skin,
Looking for water to cook her bee's honey.
Healer, with remedies that her grandmother
   taught her.

4
Para mandar lo malo pa' fuera, fuera, fuera,
Con fuego y candela limpiando toda la tierra.
Con agua y leña lo que practica nos enseña,
Salvando la selva y los ríos de pureza.
To send the bad away, away, away,
With fire and light she cleans the Earth.
With water and firewood she teaches us
   what she practices,
Saving the purity of the forest and
   the rivers.

"El Botellón" comes from the Pacific region of Colombia. I first heard it from a recording of marimba group the Grupo Naidy. They said in their liner notes that the song is used during funeral services for children, who are believed to have pure souls and ascend straight to heaven.

I've heard from other Colombians that some *bunde* funeral music is used to entertain young people during wakes while their parents mourn, and that songs like this have passed on to become everyday songs for kids.

The simplicity of this tune lends itself to many approaches, including spoken word rapping in the middle. I'm finding more and more that in settings where young people are invited to jump into the mix and get creative, singing isn't always the strongest option for everyone. However, there are highly imaginative and gifted rappers around every corner, and without a doubt, they're operating within a time-honored folk tradition. Sometimes the simplest songs give people the most room to do their thing. These days I look for any opportunity to include rapping in the middle of songs, and if that doesn't happen, an extended percussion break can be just what the tune needs. *

LISTEN . . .
Marioneta by La Cumbiamba eNeYé

¡Arriba Suena Marimba! by Grupo Naidy

La Candela Viva by Totó la Momposina

READ . . .
South American Folkloric Music: A Definitive Anthology compiled by Bill Desailly

A Different Mirror: A History of Multicultural America by Ronald Takaki

MIDNIGHT TRAIN

SONGS OF **CHILDHOOD** & **MORNING DREAMS**

FOOLISHNESS AND TRIUMPH

People say that chocolates or good conversations or ocean sunsets open the heart. This may be true, but songs do it too, and with a longlasting impact that allows the world to grow and attain new social dimensions previously unknown. Chocolate rarely has this effect.

Memories are made, movements are created and maintained. The threads that weave together to form our lives are musical threads in so many ways. I stopped trying to imagine a world without music, because it'll never happen. No wall is high enough, no river is deep enough to keep the songs from finding their way to us, usually when we need them most.

Songs of resistance, love, hunger, pain, foolishness, and triumph. Songs of terracotta and steel, dry branches and overcoats, mangos and cardboard. Songs, like loose floorboards, always awake and ready to let you know they're there.

But what are the songs without singers to belt them out for the world (or at least the neighbors) to hear? There are as many ways to sing songs as there are voices to take them on. Maybe it used to be enough to read the words on the page and ride the melody to the end. These are new days and the old songs may need some different energy. Maybe the young people need to take these songs and make them their own. Maybe we older folks can show how we used to do it and stand aside. Maybe we can create conditions in which the songs can rise again. Maybe we need to cook the soup, set the table, tune a few instruments, and step back. Maybe we can offer harmonies. Or just clap. Creating conditions for the songs to come alive and soar could be a full-time job!

It's my hope that this book will lead you to some music that turns you on and pulls you in. Maybe music that blows your mind like it did mine. I've tried to show you the songs as I play them and give you at least a few other directions to run in, there are so many ways to go. It's my hope that you come to see these songs as traveling companions, not just because of the artistry but because in times of struggle, in times of celebration, in times of war, and in times of peace songs can bring us closer to each other . . . isn't that what we wanted all along?

JANE AND LOUISA

This collection isn't exactly stuffed to the brim with waltzes, but the ones that are here have a great deal of meaning and depth. I learned this from a group of Caribbean women known as the Sandy Girls. I mention them a few times in this book because their performances were unforgettable and because they were so important to my understanding of Caribbean folk music.

This song made its way onto a record by another inspiration, the Jamaican master of ceremonies (MC) Wayne Rhoden, a.k.a. Rankin Don, a.k.a. Father Goose. Wayne was very active in the dance hall scene in Brooklyn when I met him in the mid-1990s. I was a freak for Jamaican music of any type, so for me this was a beautiful musical friendship—two shy guys record hunting, telling tall tales, and drinking ginger beer.

Soon after my daughter was born, I decided to take a few weeks and record a twelve-song cassette tape of all-ages music for the neighborhood families before scurrying back to finish recording my pop music solo album. Sheryl Crow lived around the corner and she came in and sang "Polly Wolly Doodle." Suzanne Vega came by too. So did the Sandy Girls. And, eventually, Rankin Don (soon to change his name to Father Goose) came by for a version of "Sunny Side of the Street." That was when I realized something new was happening. This was music I'd never heard before—old traditions, new personalities—it was a relaxed, modern-day mashup for an audience I'd never considered before becoming a dad.

I had dreams of Rock Glory, but God had other plans. No one cared about my major-label "comeback record" (it completely flopped!), but everybody wanted more copies of this cassette tape for families, which I called *Rocket Ship Beach*. And it was Father Goose and the music we made together—a WASP from New Hampshire and a Jamaican dance hall Don from Brooklyn—that told me all things were possible in this wild and unchartered world of twenty-first-century, all-ages social music.

Eventually, Father Goose put out a solo record for families, still considered a stone classic, called *Bam Bam Diddly*. "Jane and Louisa" is on that record. ✳

LISTEN . . .

Bam Bam Diddly by Father Goose

Feel Like Jumping: The Best of Studio One Women by various artists

Quintessential Techniques: Reggae Anthology by Winston Riley

READ . . .

Brown Girl in the Ring: An Anthology of Song Games from the Eastern Caribbean by Alan Lomax, J. D. Elder, and Bess Lomax Hawes

Brown Girl Dreaming by Jacqueline Woodson

Backyard Waltz Energy

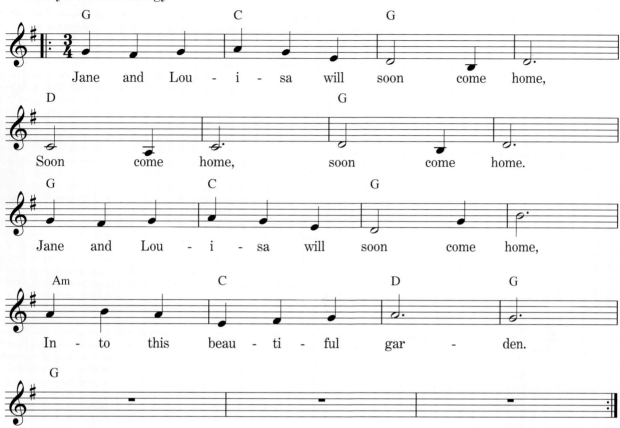

Jane and Lou – i – sa will soon come home,

Soon come home, soon come home.

Jane and Lou – i – sa will soon come home,

In – to this beau – ti – ful gar – den.

2 My dear, will you allow me to pick a rose,
Pick a rose, pick a rose?
My dear, will you allow me to pick a rose,
Into this beautiful garden?

3 My dear, will you allow me to waltz with you,
Waltz with you, waltz with you?
My dear, will you allow me to waltz with you,
Into this beautiful garden?

4 Jane and Louisa will soon come home, darling,
Soon come home, darling, soon come home.
Jane and Louisa will soon come home,
Into this beautiful garden.

Traditional, arranged by Dan Zanes. Published by Sister Barbara Music (ASCAP).
From *It's A Bam Bam Diddly!* by Father Goose.

THE RATTLIN' BOG

We recorded this with Father Goose too. He went a little off script. Here's what happened:

And on that limb there was a nest . . .
And in that nest there was a goose . . .
And on that goose there was a hat . . .
And on that hat there was a fish . . .
And on that fish there was a clock . . .
And on that clock there was a puppet . . .

It could have gone on forever, but the branch broke under the weight and it all fell to the ground!

This is one of the many communal comic songs from Ireland. It's been around for generations and there are multiple variations, including "The Everlasting Circle," "The Green Grass Grew All Around," and "The Tree on the Hill." It's what's known as a cumulative song. Other brain-stretching examples are "Alouette" and my favorite, "The Barley Mow." Things add up (and frequently speed up!), and the singers need to keep track as the list gets longer and longer. Cumulative songs are social music through and through.

There are a few different ways to approach "The Rattlin' Bog." The group can stick to the routine and sing the standard lyrics outlined here. They have some logic but also some mystery. Another approach that can be very enjoyable (and mentally taxing!) is to have people take turns picking random items to put in the nest. I've seen rocket ships, elephants, fish eyes, shoelaces, pickles, and bathrooms all end up in there. Eventually, the branch breaks, of course.

Here's another idea: If there's someone around who can paint quickly, why not set up an easel with a large sheet of paper and see if they can illustrate the song as it's being sung? I've seen Donald Saaf do this, and it never gets old. ✳

LISTEN . . .

Across the Broad Atlantic by The Wolfe Tones

Liam Clancy, self-titled

Definitive Pub Songs Collection by the Dubliners (They're all great, though!)

The Clancy Brothers and Tommy Makem, self-titled on Tradition Records

. . . and Seamus Kennedy. He's made many live comedy and music albums, and they all work!

READ . . .

Last Night's Fun: A Book About Irish Traditional Music by Ciaran Carson

A History of Irish Music by Larry Kirwan

With High Spirits

Chorus:			

Hi ho, the rat - tlin' bog, The bog down in the val - ley - o.

Hi ho, the rat - tlin' bog, The bog down in the val - ley - o.

And in that bog, there was a tree,

Rare tree rat - tlin' tree.

Tree in the bog and The bog down in the val - ley - o.

2 And on that tree there was a limb,
Rare limb a rattlin' limb.
Limb on the tree and the tree in the bog,
And the bog down in the valley-o.

3 Well on that limb there was a nest . . .

4 Now in that nest there was a bird . . .

5 In that bird there was an egg . . .

6 In that egg there was a bird . . .

Traditional, arranged by Dan Zanes. Published by Sister Barbara Music (ASCAP).
From *Night Time!* by Dan Zanes and Friends.

JUMP UP

When I was a young teenager, punk rock made its way to New Hampshire. I needed some youth energy that invited me to join in and there it was. Punk told me that I could do this music thing too, that I didn't need to have incredible chops to play in a band. I could take what I had and make it work. I needed that! All my life I'd felt as though the good times with other musicians were just out of reach. I'd be working extra hard at the guitar for months on end, and one of my classmates would pick one up and be playing Aerosmith songs within a week. It was frustrating, to say the least.

So, the idea that punk offered—that I could start with attitude and go from there—was full of the hope that I needed. Eventually, I realized that the folk singers of my childhood had been making the same case for musical inclusion, but I'd forgotten all about it in the bombastic electric '70s. It's hard to recall the words of Ramblin' Jack Elliott when just down Route 93 Pink Floyd is decorating their Boston stage with huge inflatable pigs!

Another thing punk rock offered was the idea that if I wanted to make things happen on the dance floor, all I had to do was jump up and down. It was called pogoing, but it was just jumping! Even I could do that! And this is where early childhood playtime and the Buzzcocks intersect. . . .

It's good to have a jumping song in the bag for the proper occasion.

If "Jump Up" is being sung, as well as danced to, it's easy to take a call-and-response approach. It might go like this:

Jump up (jump up), day is breaking
Jump up (jump up), let's get shaking
I know (I know) you're lying down
(Everybody) Jump up and we'll dance around! ✱

LISTEN . . .

As much as I love English punk rock—The Clash, The Jam, X-Ray Spex—I find that the English two-tone second-generation ska bands have stood the test of time for all-ages listening (and besides who doesn't love interracial music making?). You can still pogo to these records:

The Specials by The Specials

Keep the Beat: The Very Best of the English Beat by The English Beat

Too Much Pressure by The Selecter

READ . . .

I don't know if these are the best books about learning to play guitar, but I like them. One way or the other, I'd suggest looking around and finding one that feels right to you. There is no shortage of books, videos, classes, and more for the beginner these days.

How to Play Guitar: Everything You Need to Know to Play the Guitar by Roger Evans

Guitar for Absolute Beginners by Daniel Emery

ONLINE . . .

Sonicjunction.com calls itself "Music Lessons from Master Artists"—and that includes me! Electronic media took away the quiet spaces in most of our lives, spaces that left room for learning a musical instrument, but Sonicjunction.com uses technology to bring us back around. Guitar, piano, ukulele, and harmonica are all taught here, mostly at the intermediate and advanced levels.

With a Hopping Feel

Jump up,   day is break-ing Jump up,   let's get shak-ing I know you're ly-ing down

Jump up and we'll dance a - round.   Jump up, bells are ring-ing I hear friends are sing-ing

Whoa yeah,   it's a cra - zy sound   Jump up and we'll dance a - round.

2 Jump up, clouds are passing
Look up, the sky is laughing
I know we'll be laughing too
Jump up, I want to dance with you.

3 Jump up, stand on your tiptoes
Reach out grab a rainbow
Turn it upside down
Jump up, and we'll dance it around.

4 Jump up, you know I love you
That's right, I love love love you
A new day is shining down
Jump up and we'll dance around
Jump up and we'll dance around.

Written by Dan Zanes. Published by Sister Barbara Music (ASCAP).
From *Family Dance* by Dan Zanes and Friends.

PIGOGO (THE PEACOCK SONG)

"Pigogo" is a song from South Africa sung in the Zulu language. I learned it from the Children of Agape Choir. The organization Keep a Child Alive, in an effort to raise awareness of the physical, social, and economic impacts of HIV in Africa, brought the group to New York around 2006.

Much as the Fisk Jubilee Singers did more than a century before, the Children of Agape highlighted a challenge and also raised money, in this case for their orphanage, Agape, which had just burned down. Watching these singers, who had never before performed publicly (yet were as musically gifted as anyone I'd ever heard), literally getting their act together was an experience I'll never forget. In New York they spent time with Alicia Keys, Angélique Kidjo, and Paul Simon and opened hearts wherever they went. They told their story for Africa, and ultimately, for all of us.

By a stroke of great fortune, this turbulent time in the lives of the Children of Agape was well documented and turned into a film called *We Are Together*.

If you're singing this with a group, it might take a few minutes to get everyone up to speed with the background vocal parts that overlap the lead vocal, but the end result will be immensely satisfying. There is so much to be learned from South African vocal traditions. ✱

WATCH . . .

We Are Together (Thina Simunye). This documentary follows the Children of Agape for three musical years of incredible ups and downs. Check out the film's soundtrack, too!

LISTEN . . .

Thina Simunye by the Children of Agape Choir

Next Stop . . . Soweto, Vol. 1–4 by various artists

READ . . .

Nelson Mandela's Favorite African Folktales by Nelson Mandela, editor

The Invisible Cure: Why We Are Losing the Fight Against AIDS in Africa by Helen Epstein

In Township Tonight!: South Africa's Black City Music and Theatre by David B. Coplan

TRANSLATION:

When I'm walking with you, Thuli,
They are calling you a peacock
Because you are proud.

Traditional, arranged by Dan Zanes. Published by Sister Barbara Music (ASCAP).
From *Catch That Train* **by Dan Zanes and Friends.**

DOWN IN THE VALLEY

This is one of the many songs from the Southern African-American game traditions that Bessie Jones helped popularize during her lifetime. Her songs were usually performed with voice and tambourine and although we've included guitar or piano chords here they're not necessary to make this a full-blown party.

"Down in the Valley" works well as a partner dance, which means it's best when kids are old enough to follow a handful of basic instructions. Three and up? Three to three hundred? Something like that!

Here's how it can go with two people (although it can easily work for three, if it needs to, so no one gets left out). Let's call them Dancers 1 and 2:

- Partners face each other and dance lower and lower during the "Down in the Valley" chorus.
- In the first verse, "Let me see you make a motion," Dancer 1 makes a crazy motion and Dancer 2 attempts an imitation.
- In the second verse, "Let me see you make another one," Dancer 2 makes a motion, which Dancer 1 imitates.
- In the third verse, "Look up to the sky now," both dancers pretend to look into the distance (although they could be flying around the room, tiptoeing, reaching for the sky, or just about any movement the song leader can think of).
- In the final verse, "Find another partner," the dancers go off and find new partners, and it all starts again! ✳

READ . . .

Step It Down: Games, Plays, Songs, and Stories from the Afro-American Heritage by Bessie Jones and Bess Lomax Hawes

We Who Believe in Freedom: Sweet Honey in the Rock . . . Still on the Journey by Bernice Johnson Reagon

LISTEN . . .

Step It Down by Bessie Jones. This comes with a detailed booklet that breaks down the songs, a perfect guide for educators wanting to use this music in the classroom.

It's Story Telling Time by Linda Goss

Sounds of the South, compiled and recorded by Alan Lomax

WATCH . . .

Pete Seeger's TV show *The Rainbow Quest.* The episode with Bessie Jones is just one of several clips of her artistry available online.

Party Rhythm Style

Down in the val - ley,___ two by two, Two by two, ba - by two by two.

Down in the val - ley,___ two by two, And then you rise, Sa - lly,___ rise.

2 Let me see you make a motion, two by two,
Two by two, baby, two by two.
Let me see you make a motion, two by two,
Rise, Sally, rise.

3 Let me see you make another one . . .

4 Look up to the sky now . . .

5 Find another partner . . .

6 Down in the valley . . .

7 Let me see you make a motion . . .

Traditional, arranged by Dan Zanes. Published by Sister Barbara Music (ASCAP).
From *House Party* by Dan Zanes and Friends.

SKIP TO MY LOU

Play parties—19th century entertainment for young people who were prohibited from dancing for religious reasons—occurred in both the African American and white communities, and although it's likely that the styles of movement were different, the general idea was the same: find creative ways to sing children's game songs and move in structured and highly enjoyable patterns. That certainly sounds like dancing, but at the time they called it something else and got away with it!

It's quite easy to find some of the old play party moves, but here are some other ways this song could be effective in an early-childhood setting.

Dance "Skip to My Lou" in a simple circle. People hold hands and move together in one direction while singing a verse to the song. When it's time for the chorus, instead of "Skip to my Lou," the lyrics could be "Crawl to my Lou" or "Fly to my Lou," etc.

If the dancers are old enough to get it together, they can all take four steps toward the center of the circle while holding hands during the first line of a verse (for example, "Lost my partner, what'll I do?"), and four steps back in time during the second line ("Lost my partner, what'll I do?"). The whole move repeats for the second half of the verse. If this sounds confusing, try counting the steps while singing and it should make sense.

This is one of those songs that can be as flexible as the crowd wants it to be. The tempo can speed up and slow down. The volume can rise and fall. Ideas can start with the song leader and quickly shift to the dancers. I've also included some Spanish and Haitian Kreyòl lyrics to illustrate just how useful "Skip to My Lou" can be for people starting to learn these languages. ✳

READ . . .
Waltz The Hall: The American Play Party by Alan L. Spurgeon

The American Play-Party Song with a Collection of Oklahoma Texts and Tunes by Benjamin Albert Botkin

LISTEN . . .
American Play Parties by Pete Seeger, Mike Seeger & Rev. Larry Eisenberg

Raffi Radio and Everything Grows by Raffi

Call and Response and Adventures in Rhythm by Ella Jenkins

Any Feel At All!

Chorus:

Hey hey, skip to my Lou, Hey hey, skip to my Lou,

Hey hey, skip to my Lou, Skip to my Lou, my dar - ling.

Lost my part - ner, what'-ll I do? Lost my part - ner, what'-ll I do?

Lost my part - ner, what'-ll I do? Skip to my Lou, my dar - ling.

SPANISH LYRICS

fly = vuela
jump = saltar
tiptoe = (caminar de) puntillas
big steps = pasos grandes
march = marchar
walk = caminar
run = correr
crawl = gatear

HAITIAN KREYÒL LYRICS

fly = vole
jump = bondi
tiptoe = sou pwet pye
big steps = gwo mache
march = mache
run = kouri
crawl = rale sou vant

2 I'll get another one prettier than you . . .

3 Little red wagon, painted blue . . .

4 Fly in the sugar bowl, shoo, fly, shoo . . .

5 Pigs in the parlor, what'll I do? . . .

6 Rats in the bread tray, how they chew . . .

7 Catch that red bird, skip to my Lou . . .

8 Can't get a red bird, a blue bird'll do . . .

9 Can't get a blue bird, a jaybird'll do . . .

Traditional, arranged by Dan Zanes. Published by Sister Barbara Music (ASCAP).
From *Lead Belly, Baby!* by Dan Zanes and Friends.

CHO*CO*LA*TE

I'd known this song as a sort of chant, not really a melodic number, until I heard a version by Sonia De Los Santos, and sure enough, there was a guitar! And a melody! And a harmonica! And it sounds great, so I included it here and asked Sonia to say a few words about it:

"This song is based on a Mexican traditional rhyme about making chocolate (roughly translated, "stir the chocolate/Your nose of peanut). There are many versions—and probably each parent sings it a little differently—but for some reason, this is the way I sing it.

"I like this song because it reminds me of when I used to make hot chocolate back home in Monterrey, Mexico, with my mom to warm us up on cold winter days (yes, even in Mexico there are some cold days!). I remember helping her stir a big clay pot full of chocolate with a *molinillo*, a traditional wooden stick, and drinking it with *pan dulce* (sweet bread). So, let's get stirring!

"Can you count with me?" ✱

READ . . .

Here are two strong songbooks for family bands
and early-childhood educators:

De Colores and Other Latin-American Folk Songs for Children

Fiestas: A Year of Latin-American Songs and Celebrations
both by José-Luis Orozco

LISTEN . . .

Mi Viaje: De Nuevo León to the New York Island by Sonia De Los Santos

Coloreando: Traditional Songs for Children in Spanish by Marta Gómez

¡Como Bien! Eat Right! by José-Luis Orozco

JOSÉ-LUIS OROZCO

Wow, this man is working hard to help America become a bilingual country!

José-Luis Orozco (1945–) has been performing in Spanish and English for young audiences since 1970. In his records, books, videos, and concerts, he connects people to the music and culture of Latin America in a soulful and relaxed way that invites everyone to the party.

When my daughter was young and I wanted to be sure there were some Spanish-language songs around, José-Luis's recordings were the first ones I found and they are still among my favorites. I was looking for the language and he delivered the culture along with it!

José-Luis says it was his time touring the world with the Mexico City Boys Choir, starting at age eight, that set him up for his life's work connecting people through music. Today he lives in California, and in many ways the country is finally catching up to this generous musical visionary. His songs are old and new, from here and there. And in addition to his work in early-childhood circles, José-Luis wrote a song that's become a folk classic for *all* ages, "Paz y Libertad."

With Young Folk Energy

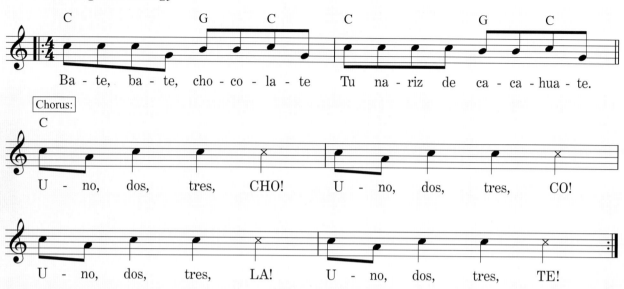

C   G   C   C   G   C

Ba - te, ba - te, cho - co - la - te   Tu na - riz de ca - ca - hua - te.

Chorus:
C

U - no, dos, tres, CHO!   U - no, dos, tres, CO!

U - no, dos, tres, LA!   U - no, dos, tres, TE!

ACCORDION

In the early 1800s, an instrument was created in Germany based on an ancient Chinese bamboo reed instrument called the *sheng*. An old idea became something new: the accordion!

An accordion moves air across metal reeds that produce different notes. The player moves air by expanding and contracting the bellows. If you blow into a harmonica, that sound of air vibrating the thin metal reeds inside is similar to the sound of an accordion, but on a much smaller scale.

Accordions have become popular around the world. They're loud! They're portable! They don't need to be tuned! They look cool! Today, accordions are a crucial part of music in many countries, including Mexico, the United States, South Africa, France, Argentina, Colombia, North Korea, Brazil, and more. Piano players should know that, as far as playing the accordion goes, you're already halfway there—many accordions have piano keys. What are you waiting for?

Traditional, arranged by Sonia De Los Santos. Published by De Los Santos Music (ASCAP).
From *Mi Viaje: De Nuevo León to the New York Island* by Sonia De Los Santos.

FOOBA WOOBA JOHN

With Ancient Comic Swing

Saw a flea kick a tree Foo - ba Woo - ba Foo - ba Woo - ba

Saw a flea kick a tree Foo - ba Woo - ba John

Saw a flea kick a tree in the mid-dle of the sea

Chorus:

Hey, John, Ho, John, Foo - ba Woo - ba John.

Interlude 1   Back to Verse

Interlude 2

Back to Verse

Traditional, arranged by Dan Zanes. Published by Sister Barbara Music (ASCAP).
From *Family Dance* by Dan Zanes and Friends.

2 Saw a frog chase a dog . . .
sitting on a hollow log

3 Saw a snail chase a whale . . .
all around the water pail

4 Heard a cow say meow . . .
then I heard it say bow wow

"Fooba Wooba John" is a member of a small but significant club: tall-tale songs from the British Isles about slightly unusual or impossible feats involving animals and insects.

A near cousin to this song, "Martin Said to His Man," can be traced back to the 1600s. In that song, things get a little psychedelic: "I saw the cheese eat the rat / Saw a mouse chase a cat," and "I saw a flea heave a tree / Twenty miles out to sea."

The form is set and the lyrics are rich, but there's plenty of room for updates. Get out the notebooks!

I recorded this song with Rosanne Cash. It was one of the most natural and enjoyable sessions I've ever had. Her approach to it was complete, comfortable, well lived-in, and funny. Since that day, I've been asking if she'll do a whole record like this. ✳

READ . . .

The Vaughan Williams Memorial Library (www.vwml.org), located in London's Cecil Sharp House, is the place to go for all of your English-language folk music needs, including the Roud Folk Song Index. Just don't plan on a quick visit. . . .

LISTEN . . .

The Little White Duck by Burl Ives

Spencer the Rover Is Alive and Well by John Roberts and Tony Barrand. This collection includes a classic version of "Martin Said to His Man."

UKULELE

The ukulele is a small hollow-body, four-string instrument usually made of wood (although plastic models have been made over the years).

Many people think of the ukulele as a Hawai'ian instrument, but its roots go back to the island of Madeira off the coast of Portugal. In the late 1800s, Portuguese laborers went to work on Hawai'ian sugar plantations. They brought an instrument with them called the *machete* or *braga*. The instrument became popular among Hawai'ians. Eventually, King Kalakaua, "the Merrie Monarch," took an interest and helped bring much attention to the instrument. Eventually, it became known as the ukulele.

In 1915 the ukulele was introduced to millions of people visiting the Hawai'ian Pavilion at the Panama-Pacific International Exposition in San Francisco. It quickly became a national craze that lasted for decades.

Despite ups and downs in popularity, the ukulele is back on top in the twenty-first century, now outselling guitars in the United States. Why are ukuleles so popular? They're easy to play! They're small and portable! They're limitless in their musical possibilities! They're social! They have a rich history! They speak to us in a language we can all understand! George Harrison played one!

ALL AROUND THE KITCHEN!

Playfully and Soulfully

Traditional, arranged by Dan Zanes. Published by Sister Barbara Music (ASCAP).
From *Family Dance* by Dan Zanes and Friends.

I added some other lyrics along the way:

2 Stop right there!
Make your arms into trees
Wave them in the breeze
Walk and wobble your knees

3 Stop right there!
Make your arms into wings
Flap those things
Fly around in a circle

When I first heard Pete Seeger play this song, I thought it was rock and roll! It was speed, it was force, it was energy, it was one chord, and . . . it was a little unhinged. It sounded like a power trio, but it was just a guy playing a banjo and singing with gusto. It felt like all my worlds mashed up into two minutes.

In my travels, I've been able to visit many spaces where kids are ready to sing and dance, and this song is *always* a dependable friend to bring along. The first recorded performance took place in Alabama in 1940. John and Ruby Lomax recorded a group of African American kids singing "All Around the Kitchen!" as a circle dance. Ruth Crawford Seeger included it in her book *American Folk Songs for Children* in 1948, and Pete Seeger released the first commercial recording of it a few years later. This song is a staple in early-childhood circles and, although it's hard to track down that original version from Alabama (the index card for the recording in the Library of Congress can easily be viewed online), it's meaningful to be able to acknowledge the song's African American roots.

The lyrics are as flexible as anyone wants them to be. A double rhyme? Sure! A triple rhyme? There's room! Dance like a bear? A snake? A tree? If people can think on their feet, that helps, but it takes almost no time at all to concoct and memorize lyrics to pull out when the moment is right. Take the cues from the crowd and follow the smiles. ✳

READ . . .

The "Music Together" early-childhood music program is available all over the place. Their songbooks have a lot of solid information.

Culturally Responsive Teaching and The Brain: Promoting Authentic Engagement and Rigor Among Culturally and Linguistically Diverse Students by Zaretta L. Hammond

LISTEN . . .

The Story That the Crow Told Me: Early American Rural Children's Songs, Vols. 1 and 2 by various artists

Vocal, Chamber, and Instrumental Works of Ruth Crawford Seeger. Maybe modernist composition and folk are closer than we think.

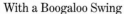

With a Boogaloo Swing

Chorus:

Po - lli -to, chick - en, Ga - lli - na, hen, Lá-
- piz, pen - cil And plu -ma, pen._ Ven - ta - na, win- dow, Y,
puer - to door, Ma - es - tra, teach-er And pi - so, floor, Po -

Con Abuelita:

lli - to, chick - en, Ga - lli - na hen,
Lá - piz, pen - cil Y plu - ma, pen. Ven -
ta - na, win - dow, Puer - ta, door, Ma -
es - tra, teach - er Y pi - so, floor.

Traditional, arranged by Dan Zanes, additional lyrics by Caridad de le Luz. Published by Sister Barbara Music (ASCAP).
From *¡Nueva York!* by Dan Zanes and Friends.

La Bruja's lyrics:

Pollito chicken comes out of his egg
That the *gallina* hen in her nest just laid
And the *lápiz* pencil a tic-tac-toe played
While *la pluma* the pen, some poetry made
Ventana window keeps out the rain
While *la puerta* the door
vOpens up for Dan Zanes! Hola!
Maestra teacher says the word of the day
On the *piso* floor we all dance and say.

Pollito chicken flies all around as the
Gallina hen picks corn from the ground
And the *lapiz* pencil writes her thoughts down
While the *pluma la* pen draws on a clown
Window *ventana* lets in the breeze
While *la puerta* the door
Slams when you sneeze
The teacher *maestra* shows how to say please
On the *piso* the floor we shake our knees

This is a nursery rhyme often quite familiar to people in Puerto Rican communities. I've heard many elders say that, as new Spanish-speaking immigrants to the United States, this was one way of communicating with their English-speaking grandchildren. Sometimes it's the other way around—the older folks use it to help their grandchildren learn to speak Spanish. Either way, everybody learns something valuable and can have a good time doing it!

It's not unusual to hear children's rhymes as the starting point for larger songs (the dance halls in Jamaica, for example, are filled with them), and that's what happened here. Caridad De la Luz, a.k.a. "La Bruja" (in English, "The Witch"), is a gifted and celebrated Nuyorican poet, rapper, actress, and educator. She took something simple and created an entire poetic "Pollito Chicken" universe. And then, right at the end, when it seems that there's no more room in the song for anything else . . . who should appear but her *abuelita* to help her with her Spanish! ✱

LISTEN . . .

For Witch It Stands by La Bruja

Folksongs of Puerto Rico and *Asi Bailaba Puerto Rico: Al Son de la Bomba y la Plena,*
both by various artists

READ . . .

My Music Is My Flag: Puerto Rican Musicians and Their New York Communities, 1917–1940
by Ruth Glasser

Grandma's Records (Los Discos de mi Abuela) by Eric Velasquez

131

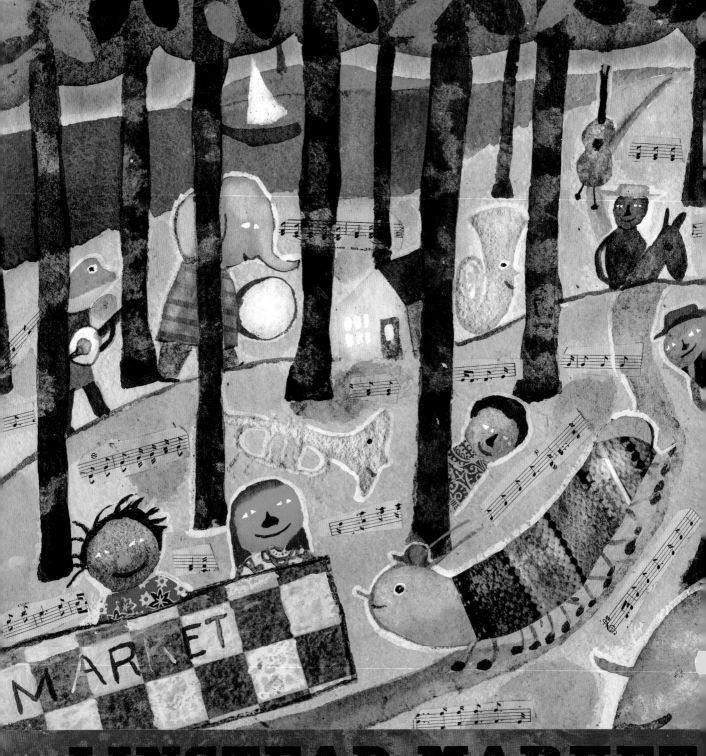

LINSTEAD MARKET

SONGS OF MYSTERY & MILES

A SUMMER NIGHT

The skies are calm and the sun is setting reluctantly in the west. Beneath the apple tree is a table long and worn. Loaves of bread are piled high. Pitchers of sorrel here and there. And then . . . the wooden bowls, so many of them! Beet greens, diri djon djon, ackee and saltfish, roast potatoes, dosas, zucchini fritters, olives, mangos, tempura, baba ganoush, green papaya salad, fattoush, fresh mozzarella, red curry, yellow curry, green curry! There's a seat for one and all. Strumming, plucking, tapping, shaking, and scraping—a musical conversation—as the songs swirl and mingle and rise above the scene. Signature songs. Dancing songs. Drinking songs. Songs of love and laughter, healing and headaches. Stories and melodies from near and far. Kreyol, Patois, Spanglish, and Ukrainian. Signing and smiling as kids run through the field in secret games of youth. As the orange sky below the trees deepens and darkens, old folks light candles and recall how quickly time slips away, while the songs lean one way and then the other, never leaving anyone behind.

TURN, TURN, TURN

As the story goes, Pete Seeger's wife, Toshi, told him that "Turn, Turn, Turn" was a beautiful song, but it would be nice if he could write some words that would be suitable for very young people (they had two small kids at the time). He said that's a great idea, why don't you try it? And she did! Toshi wrote five perfect verses that sat in a notebook for over fifty years until Pete rediscovered them a few years before he passed away in 2014. At that time, he began singing them at concerts. That's the story I heard and I love it.

Toshi Seeger died in 2013 at the age of ninety-one. Their seventieth wedding anniversary was just nine days away. The memories that people shared made one thing very clear: No Toshi, no Pete. By all accounts (including his, always), she gave him more than just the structure and the foundation to do what he did. In an interview for Mountain Lake PBS after Toshi died, Pete said, "She was the brains in our family. I might get an idea for something, but she'd figure out how to make it work."

There are a lot of men mentioned and represented in this humble songbook. It's difficult to imagine almost any of them doing what they did without strong support from a partner (or partners) in life. The legends tell us of the rugged individuals who go out and conquer the world, but hats off to Pete Seeger for letting us in on the real story. And thank you to Toshi Seeger for a lifetime of environmental activism, filmmaking, family, and groundbreaking festival production. And for these five incredible verses, now liberated from a dusty old notebook. ✱

WATCH . . .
Afro-American Work Songs in a Texas Prison **(1966)** by Toshi Seeger, Daniel Seeger, Peter Seeger, and Bruce Jackson

READ . . .
Pete Seeger's Storytelling Book by Pete Seeger and Paul Dubois Jacobs

Pete Seeger in His Own Words selected and edited by Rob Rosenthal and Sam Rosenthal

Henscratches and Flyspecks: How to Read Melodies from Songbooks in Twelve Confusing Lessons by Pete Seeger

Carry It On: The Story of America's Working People in Song and Picture by Pete Seeger and Bob Reiser

LISTEN . . .
American Favorite Ballads, Vols. 1–5, ***American Folk, Game, and Activity Songs***, ***Birds, Beasts, Bugs & Fishes Little & Big***, and ***The Complete Carnegie Hall Concert June 8, 1963***, all by Pete Seeger

Strong and Thoughtful

Toshi Seeger's Lyrics:

2
A time to dress, A time to eat
A time to sit and rest your feet
A time to teach, A time to learn
A time for all to take their turn

3
A time to cry and make a fuss
A time to leap and catch the bus
A time for quiet, A time for talk
A time to run, A time to walk

4
A time to get, A time to give
A time to remember, A time to forgive
A time to hug, A time to kiss
A time to close your eyes and wish

5
A time for dirt, A time for soap
A time for tears, A time for hope
A time for fall, A time for spring
A time to hear the robins sing

Pete Seeger, Toshi Seeger. Melody Trails, Inc. (BMI).
From *Turn Turn Turn* by Dan Zanes and Elizabeth Mitchell with You Are My Flower.

HILL AND GULLY RIDER

Jamaica has produced music is some of the best loved music in the world. This folk song has appeared with a few different sets of lyrics over the years and has been embraced by singers in many of the island's styles. The lyrics refer to the landscape—there are hills and valleys, up and down, high and low. A hill and gully rider travels through it all!

Mento music, the precursor to ska, is discussed in this book with the song "Go Down Emmanuel Road." "Hill and Gully Rider" was played by many mento performers, most notably Lord Composer. One of the interesting things about this song is its appeal over the generations and across genres—mento to ska to rocksteady to reggae to dance hall. The Charms, Tommy McCook and his Skatalites, Lovindeer, Johnny Osbourne, Ini Kamoze, Yellowman, Ernie Smith, Joseph Cotton, and The Gaylads all recorded lively versions that speak to the remarkable creativity of Jamaican musicians and to the importance of folk music in Jamaican popular culture.

Once upon a time, I learned a simple but totally enjoyable dance to this song in a book that was inspired by Hungarian composer Zoltán Kodály. The dance looks something like this:

Hill and gully rider (take four steps forward with the music)
Hill and gully (clap four times with the words)
Hill and gully rider (take four steps back with the music)
Hill and gully (clap four times
with the words)

During the verse lines, dancers take quarter turns to the right, always stopping to clap four times with the "Hill and gully" answer. On the page it doesn't look like much, but in real life it's an instant party. ✳

LISTEN . . .

John Crow Say: Jamaican Music of Faith, Work, and Play by various artists

Songs from Jamaica by Edric Connor and The Caribbeans. This record by the Trinidad-born English singer has many of the Jamaican folk songs people know and love. It's some good folk music one-stop shopping.

READ . . .

Wake the Town and Tell the People: Dancehall Culture in Jamaica by Norman C. Stolzoff

Kodály Today: A Cognitive Approach to Elementary Music Education by Mícheál Houlahan and Philip Tacka

Late Night Groove
Intro in C

Chorus:
Hill and gull-y ri-der (Hill and gull-y) Hill and gull-y ri-der (Hill and gull-y) I took my

horse an' com-in' down (Hill and gull-y) but my horse done stum-ble down (Hill and gull-y) An' the

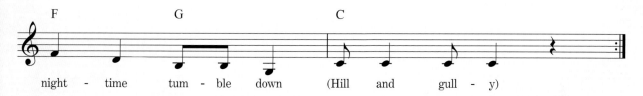

night - time tum - ble down (Hill and gull - y)

2 Oh, the moon shone bright down
(Hill and gully)
Ain't no place for hiding down
(Hill and gully)
An' a zombie come a riding down
(Hill and gully)

3 Oh, my knees they shake down
(Hill and gully)
An' my heart starts quaking down
(Hill and gully)
An' I run 'til daylight breaking down
(Hill and gully)

4 Well that's the last I sat down
(Hill and gully)
I pray the Lord don't let me down
(Hill and gully)
Ain't nobody going to get me down
(Hill and gully)

**"What is universally human can
be approached by all peoples
only through their specific, national
characteristics."** —Zoltan Kodály

Traditional, arranged by Dan Zanes. Published by Sister Barbara Music (ASCAP).
From *Little Nut Tree* by Dan Zanes and Friends.

LOCH LOMOND

There's a lot to say about this one. For our purposes I've decided to present a common version of the song and a common version of the story behind it, although, because there are so many different opinions about its history, I encourage anyone who's curious to go on and dig. The results will be illuminating.

As one story goes, during the Jacobite Rebellion of 1745, Charles Edward Stuart, a.k.a. "Bonnie Prince Charles," led his soldiers from Scotland to England in an attempt to restore Scottish rule to Great Britain. The song describes the story of two Scottish soldiers captured in the Battle of Carlisle. One was sentenced to death and one was to be set free. According to Scottish Gaelic lore, one who dies outside the country will be transported home by "faeries" through an underground passageway known as the low road. The soldier in the song who is about to die is telling his comrade that they'll meet again in Scotland and, because he's going to be carried by faeries, he'll get there first.

There are also numerous Scottish terms used in the song. A "brae" is a hillside, a "loch" is a lake, a "ben" is a mountain, and "bonnie" means pretty.

It's a song of sadness, no doubt, yet it's also a song of mystery, and therefore a song for all ages. The chorus is uplifting, open to interpretation, and certainly ready for some down-tempo gusto. This is a perfect way to end a long evening of neighborhood music making. ✳

READ . . .

Mudcat.org is the place to go for all your most pressing historical folk music needs. The threads are long and often—as in the case of "Loch Lomond"—very deep. It's a gathering place for hardcore enthusiasts to ask questions and share knowledge.

LISTEN . . .

The Jacobite Rebellions by Ewan MacColl

So Many Partings and *Kiss the Tears Away,* both by Silly Wizard

The Mermaid's Song and *Land of Light,* both by The Tannahill Weavers

With a Long, Walking Pace

By yon bon-nie banks,   by yon bon-nie braes Where the sun shines bright on Loch Lo - mond Where

me and my true love were ev - er want to be On the bon-nie, bon-nie banks of Loch Lo - mond.

Chorus:

You take the high road and I'll take the low road I'll be in Scot-land be - fore you But

me and my true love will nev - er meet a-gain On the bon-nie, bon-nie banks of Loch Lo - mond.

2 Mind where we parted in yon shady glen
On the steep, steep side of Ben Lomond
Where in deep purple hues the Highland hills
   we viewed
And the moon coming out in the gloaming.

3 The wee birdies sing and the wild
   flowers spring
And the sunshine and the waters are sleeping
The broken heart it kens, no second
   Spring again
And the world does not know how we're
   greeting.

Traditional, arranged by Dan Zanes. Published by Sister Barbara Music (ASCAP).
From *Catch That Train* **by Dan Zanes and Friends.**

GOODBYE, OLD PAINT

"To know that an iconic song like 'Goodbye Old Paint' was learned from a black cowboy speaks a lot of the strength and influence black cowboys had on western culture . . . their existence opens a bigger conversation on the multicultural nature of the West."

—Dom Flemons, *The American Songster*

This song was popular among the cowboys who worked driving cattle during the 1800s. The labor was hard, so after-hours amusements were important. Much like contra dances in New England, cowboy dances commonly ended with a waltz. According to song collector and cowboy historian John Lomax, "Goodbye, Old Paint" replaced "Home Sweet Home" as the parting number during these "shindigs." ("Paint" refers to a breed of horse with a spot pattern.)

Although mainstream information about cowboys is plentiful, usually the story is only half told. Approximately one in four cowboys from the mid- to late 1800s was African American. That's a lot of black cowboys! And it wasn't just men—African American women were very much involved in the work during the westward expansion. I wish I had learned the real history when I was a kid. Folk and blues musician Lead Belly spent much of his youth in Texas and was undoubtedly aware of this history. He even went to Hollywood at one point to seek work as a black cowboy in films. Unfortunately for all of us, it didn't work out for him.

This is one of those songs that can be as flexible as people want it to be. It's said that in the days of the cowboys, the dance would go on as long as people could improvise new lyrics! This versatility also makes it a great one to sing with children. Leaving Cheyenne? Leaving New York? Leaving the house? In my copy of *American Folk Songs for Children*, a teacher wrote in the margins, "Good to sing before going home (while putting on boots). Makes them forget unhappiness." ✳

LISTEN . . .

Dom Flemons Presents Black Cowboys by Dom Flemons

High Lonesome Cowboy by Don Edwards and Peter Rowan

Cowboy Songs on Folkways by various artists

READ . . .

The Black West: A Documentary and Pictorial History of the African American Role in the Westward Expansion of the United States by William Loren Katz

Black Cowboys in the American West: On the Range, on the Stage, Behind the Badge by Bruce A. Glasrud and Michael N. Searles, editors

Dusty, Flowing Waltz
Intro in A

Good - bye, old Paint, I'm leav - ing Chey - enne. Good -
bye, old Paint, I'm leav - ing Chey - enne. Old
Paint's a good po - ny, He runs when he can.___ Good
mor - ning, young la - dy, My po - ny won't stand___ Good -

2 I'm riding old Paint
And I'm leading old Tan.
Good morning, little Annie,
I'm off for Montan'.

3 Oh hitch up your horses
And feed them some hay.
Seat yourself by me
As long as you stay.

4 My wagon is loaded
And rolling away.
My horses ain't hungry,
They'll not eat your hay.

5 My foot's in the stirrup,
My pony won't stand.
I'm a-leavin' Cheyenne,
I'm off for Montan' . . .

Traditional, arranged by Dan Zanes. Published by Sister Barbara Music (ASCAP).
From *Rocket Ship Beach* by Dan Zanes and Friends.

DAME LA MANO PALOMA

With Wild Party Energy

Da - me__ la ma - no, pa - lo - ma__

Pa - ra__ su - bir a tu ni - do.__ ni - do__

Que me han di - cho que estás so - la, Que_ me han di - cho que estás

so - la a - com - pa - ñar - te he ve - ni - do__

Que me han di - cho que estás so - la, Que_ me han di - cho que estás

so - la a - com - pa - ñar - te he ve - ni - do__

2. Cuando yo voy a Borinquen,
No puedo ir caminando. [2x]
Pero a lo largo del vuelo,
Pero a lo largo del vuelo, mi corazón va
cantando. [2x]

When I go to Borinquen,
I cannot go walking. [2x]
But when I fly to the island,
But when I fly to the island my heart sings
all the way there. [2x]

Traditional, arranged by Dan Zanes. Published by Sister Barbara Music (ASCAP).
From ¡Nueva York! by Dan Zanes and Friends.

3

Cuando yo toco guitarra,
Siento una gran alegría. [2x]
Canta y baila todo el mundo,
Canta y baila todo el mundo en
    perfecta armonía. [2x]

When I play my guitar,
I feel a great joy. [2x]
Everybody sing and dance,
Everybody sing and dance in
*   perfect harmony. [2x]*

4

Cuando llegue el año nuevo,
Yo quiero estar a tu lado. [2x]
Para darte el primero beso,
Para darte el primer beso del año
    que ha comenzado. [2x]

When the new year arrives,
I want to be by your side. [2x]
To give you the first kiss,
To give you the first kiss of the
*   year that's just begun. [2x]*

This is another winner from Puerto Rico! When we recorded a CD called *Nueva York* in 2008, the idea was to present a party—*our* party. The national "conversation" about immigration was getting uglier and uglier, and much of the talk was directed at the Latinx communities here in the United States. I thought about myself as a kid growing up in New Hampshire, and how the news of the outside world could feel so frightening. It could easily have the effect of making me hesitant to try to connect with people who didn't look and sound like me!

If we made a record that reflected the fun we were having in real life—Colombians, Mexicans, Dominicans, Puerto Ricans, Cubans, Americans, all singing, jamming, eating, laughing, and just hanging out together—maybe the kid in Nebraska who was hearing a stream of negative talk coming out of the TV and radio (or at the dinner table, for that matter) would be able to consider this alternative: life's possibilities are rich and unlimited when we're all in this thing together.

"Dame La Mano Paloma" is a festive song that people sing during the Christmas holidays in Puerto Rico. Often, neighbors go from house to house with their late-night musical merrymaking, known as *parrandas*. I wish this experience for all of you. And if you didn't have one before, now you have a song to sing. Improvised verses are welcomed. And so is food. ✱

LISTEN . . .

Mi Cantar Criollo by Antonio Cabán Vale "El Topo"

Viva Puerto Rico Libre: A Collection of the Most Important Contemporary Songs of the Independence Movement by various artists

Rafael Hernandez, Vols. 1–2 by Rafael Hernández

Vamos de Parranda by Victoria Sanabria

READ . . .

Puerto Rican Pioneers in Jazz, 1900–1939: Bomba Beats to Latin Jazz by Basilio Serrano

¡Musica!: The Rhythm of Latin America by Sue Steward

Through the Eyes of Rebel Women: The Young Lords, 1969–1976 by Iris Morales

Latin Jazz: The Perfect Combination by Raúl Fernández

143

BEAUTIFUL ISLE OF SOMEWHERE

This song is based on a poem called "Beautiful Isle" written by Jessie Brown Pounds in 1896. The following year John Sylvester Fearis put it to music.

These were the days before phonograph players and radios spread recorded music far and wide. Wax cylinders had been invented and were being produced to some degree, but for listeners wanting to hear a popular song, the common thing to do was buy the sheet music and play it at home. At this point in time, it was generally middle- and upper-class people who had access to pianos and the time to learn to play them. "Beautiful Isle of Somewhere" was sung at President William McKinley's funeral in 1901. The song became wildly popular and was played frequently at funerals for the next several decades.

I learned this song from my brother-in-law, Donald Saaf. Along the way he changed a few lyrics around to suit his needs, and I've left those changes, as well as the original lyrics, in italics . . . take your pick!

This song is often presented as a smooth-sounding, easy-listening piece. There certainly is comfort in that presentation, but it's not all silk and stainless steel. There are the edges here: the lyrics speak to frayed tablecloths, squeaking floorboards, chicken feathers, and a longing for something more. There's a hope that morning dreams and spiritual power will help us find our way to that place, and I believe they will. ✳

LISTEN . . .

The University of California at Santa Barbara Cylinder Audio Archive. Thousands of wax cylinders are archived and digitized for your listening pleasure at www.cylinders.library.ucsb.edu.

READ . . .

Close Harmony: A History of Southern Gospel by James R. Goff. Although this book doesn't cover exactly the tradition that "Beautiful Isle of Somewhere" comes out of, it details the rise of white gospel music, an important branch of the tree.

Slow, Graceful Waltz

Some-where the sun is shin - ing, Some-where the song - birds dwell;

Hush, then, thy sad re - pin - ing, there's some-place where all____ is well.

Chorus:

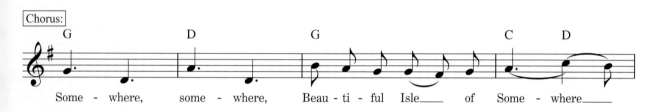

Some - where, some - where, Beau - ti - ful Isle____ of Some - where____

Land of the true, where we live____ a - new, Beau - ti - ful Is - le of Some - where.

2
Somewhere the day is longer,
Somewherae the task is done;
Somewhere the heart is stronger,
Somewhere the guerdon won
(Somewhere the prize is won)

3
Somewhere the load is lifted,
Close by an open gate;
Somewhere the clouds are rifted,
Somewhere the angels wait.
(Somewhere our friends all wait)

Public Domain, arranged by Dan Zanes. Published by Sister Barbara Music (ASCAP).
From *Little Nut Tree* by Dan Zanes and Friends.

DEEP BLUE  SEA

"What's good about folk music is that it is not show business. . . . Folk music should be part of everyday life and should help keep it from being drab." —Pete Seeger

The origins of this song have always been somewhat unclear. Pete Seeger popularized it in the mid-1950s and suggested it was cobbled together from English seafaring songs and Caribbean folk tunes. Well, all right!

It's an ideal song for social music making. If the listener isn't familiar with it at the start, they certainly will be as soon as they hit the middle of the second verse. That's part of the reason it's included here. In addition to the poetry of the lyrics, the melody is simple enough that harmony parts are easy—and harmony singing is such a beautiful part of musical life!

I spent the first half of my life wishing I could sing harmonies and the second half actually working on it. For the longest time, I wanted to skip the beginner stages and go straight to where I'd sound pretty impressive. All that really happened with that attitude was . . . well, nothing! I was too uptight to try and learn. Eventually, I made some friends who were in the same boat and we started playing together every Tuesday night. Old-time North American folk and 1950s rock and roll were our vehicles and slowly, in our own fumbling way, we started working out a sound. We gave ourselves a name, the String Kings, and booked a gig at the West Village Nursing Home.

The atmosphere with this crew was always supportive, and there was absolutely no pressure to get to the Top of the Pops. The goal was to have fun, improve as players and singers, and eventually share whatever it was we cooked up with our neighbors. Social music was our bag, and "Deep Blue Sea" was one of our "hits." ✱

LISTEN . . .
The Deighton Family. This group recorded only three albums, but they're all classics. They had a raggedy spirit that was pure joy, and the String Kings wanted to be just like them!

Jamaican Folk Songs by Louise Bennett

READ . . .
Pete Seeger: In His Own Words, edited by Rob Rosenthal and Sam Rosenthal

How to Play the 5-String Banjo by Pete Seeger

Slowly or Up-tempo

Deep blue sea, ba-by, deep blue sea

Deep blue sea, ba-by, deep blue sea

Deep blue sea, ba-by, deep blue sea

Chorus:

It was Will-y___ what got drown-ed in the deep blue sea.

2 Dig his grave with a silver spade . . .

3 Lower him down with a golden chain . . .

4 Wrap him up with a silken shroud . . .

5 Golden sun bring him back to me . . .

Traditional, arranged by Dan Zanes. Published by Sister Barbara Music (ASCAP).
From _Sea Music_ by Dan Zanes and Friends.

SIYAHAMBA

With Uplifting Spirit

Si - ya - hamb - a, eku-kan-yen' ni kwen-kos',___ Si - ya -

hamb - a, eku-kan-yen' ni kwen-kos',___ Si - ya -

hamb - a, eku-kan-yen' ni kwen-kos',___ Si - ya -

ham - ba, eku-kan-yen' ni kwen-kos', Si - ya -

ham - ba,___ si - ya - ham - ba,___ Si - ya -

ham - ba, eku-kan-yen' ni kwen-kos'. Si - ya -

ham - ba,___ si - ya - ham - ba,___ Si - ya -

ham - ba, eku-kan-yen' ni kwen-kos'.___

148 LINSTEAD MARKET

Traditional, arranged by Dan Zanes Published by Sister Barbara Music (ASCAP).
From *Night Time!* by Dan Zanes and Friends.

2 We are marching in the light of God,
We are marching in the light of God,
We are marching in the light of God,
We are marching in the light of God.

3 We are marching, we are marching, oh,
We are marching in the light of God.
We are marching, we are marching, oh,
We are marching in the light of God.

"Addictions, racism, prejudice, wealth, and social status are among those things that keep us from being free. There is also the reality that many in our own society do not enjoy economic security and other freedoms that accompany others. We all need to sing songs of liberation."

— C. Michael Hawn, Professor of Church Music, Southern Methodist University, Dallas. He wrote extensively about "Siyahamba."

LISTEN . . .

South African Music Archive Project, www.samap.ukzn.ac.za

The Holy Cross Choir, Lusanda Spiritual Group, and the Soweto Gospel Choir (All feature some beautiful choir sounds and songs.)

Mbube Roots: Zulu Choral Music from South Africa, 1930s–1960s by various artists

1979 by Fjedur

Freedom is Coming by Fjedur and Vred Fred

READ . . .

African Composers Edition (african-composers-edition.co.za) specializes in online scores from historical and contemporary African composers.

South African singers! Swedish singers! The '70s! The song! In 1978, the Lutheran Church of Sweden Mission sponsored a trip by Anders Nyberg and his vocal group, Fjedur, to South Africa. There, they performed their choral music and heard songs of the country (like South Africa, Sweden developed strong acapella choral traditions in the twentieth century), including the Zulu folk song "Siyahamba." As anyone likely would, they flipped! Fjedur began performing it around Scandinavia, and in 1984, Nyberg published *Freedom Is Coming: Songs of Protest and Praise from South Africa*, which introduced "Siyahamba" to the rest of the world. It has since become a wildly popular choral song for groups large and small.

I first heard this from a friend's vocal group named Patchwork, when they came to cut some songs in my basement studio years ago. I was learning how to use my eight-track recording gear and they needed a demo tape. No money changed hands, and I received something much more valuable than dough: an introduction to this song! I hadn't even heard it through to the end and knew I'd be singing it myself, which is, I imagine, how people everywhere feel when they hear "Siyahamba." Since that evening, I've heard dozens, if not hundreds, of versions and, in one way or another, they all offer the promise of community and liberation. ✱

WHILE THE MUSIC IS PLAYING

With a Sense of Possibility

Peo-ple gath-er all a-round the square   Hear the laugh-ing in the eve-ning air

Swirl,   and min-gle with the   songs   that brought us   there___   brought us all___

there   Ev-ery bod-y spread their   lawn chairs 'round

Out   on   the   grass   the   stars   shine   down

Karl   King's   big   brass   band___   plays that   cir - cus   sound___

___   cir - cus   sound___   And

Chorus:

I don't want to go   home_   Can we stay right   here   for a   cou-ple more songs?

I   don't want to go home___ while the mu-sic is play-ing,   Oh,_while it's play-ing

Written by Dan Zanes. Published by Sister Barbara Music (ASCAP).
From *Catch That Train* by Dan Zanes and Friends.

2 Everybody spread their lawn chairs 'round
   Out on the grass and the stars shine down
   Karl King's big brass band
   Plays that circus sound, the circus sound.

3 Every summer when the corn is high
   There's a weekend when the streets are lined
   With hot-rod cars driven in
   From another time, another time.

4 And every car has got the radio on
   Golden oldies and we're singing along
   Dancing on the sidewalk
   To those Drifters' songs, Marvelettes' songs.

5 'Round the campfire, faces glow
   The Gonzales brothers came here so
   We're singing all of the songs
   That everyone knows, everyone knows.

This song is about a trip that changed my life. The University of Iowa in Iowa City invited me to spend three weeks traveling and singing my way through small towns in the state. I thought I knew what to expect, but I was wrong! I thought it was going to look like a flatter version of my mostly white birthplace, New Hampshire, but instead what I saw on my trip was a rapidly evolving demographic. Many Mexican and Central American people had recently arrived, mainly due to meatpacking jobs. Some towns that I visited went from almost no Latinx families to thirty or forty percent of the local population within a generation! In some communities the welcome mat was clearly in place, and the people were working it out. In others, there was suspicion and fear among the longtime residents. I could feel the different climates in the towns almost immediately.

But everywhere, regardless of what was going on, there was a sense that it was all up for grabs. Young white and brown people were going to school together. Bread was being broken and bread was ready to be broken. The generosity of everyone I met—Mexican, white American, Central American, old, young, longtime residents, new neighbors—was inspiring and eye-opening. We sang, laughed, talked, ate, and shared whatever else there was to share

I came back to New York and started taking Spanish classes at El Taller in East Harlem. I began meeting new friends and hearing new stories. The biases I'd developed from the earliest years, the walls around my mind and heart that had kept me ignorant for so long, began to crumble. I started to read more and to ramble farther and farther from my comfortable neighborhood. I began to reimagine life's wild possibilities for myself and others. I had to go to small towns in Iowa to learn what had been right in front of me all along in New York: when it's a choice between love and fear, love will always throw the best party. ✳

Chord diagrams are easy to figure out. Each vertical line (from left to right) corresponds with one string on the guitar or ukulele (from top to bottom as you're holding the instrument). The black dots show where your fingers press down on the strings to create a chord. Open circles at the top of the diagram, together with the black dots, indicate strings that should be strummed. An "x" tells you a string should not be strummed.

The chords for each song in this book are shown as letters above the musical staffs. Some chords are more difficult than others, as are some changes from one chord to another. Have patience . . . it takes time. Your fingertips may even hurt a little at first if you're new to stringed instruments, but soon you'll get the hang of it!

Finally, these chords are by no means all the chords out there, but they do represent the majority used in this book. If you're curious and want to learn more chords, there's a ton of resources on the internet.

GUITAR CHORDS

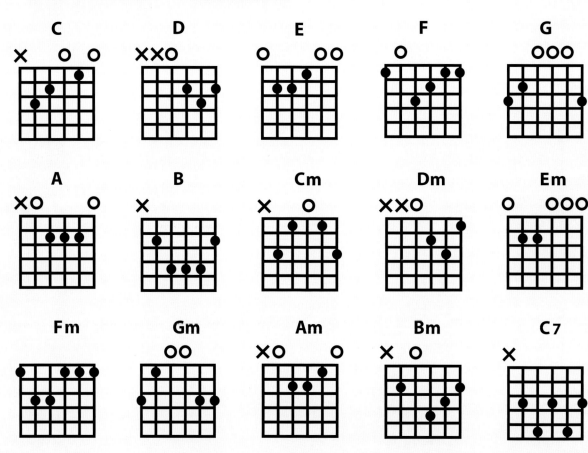

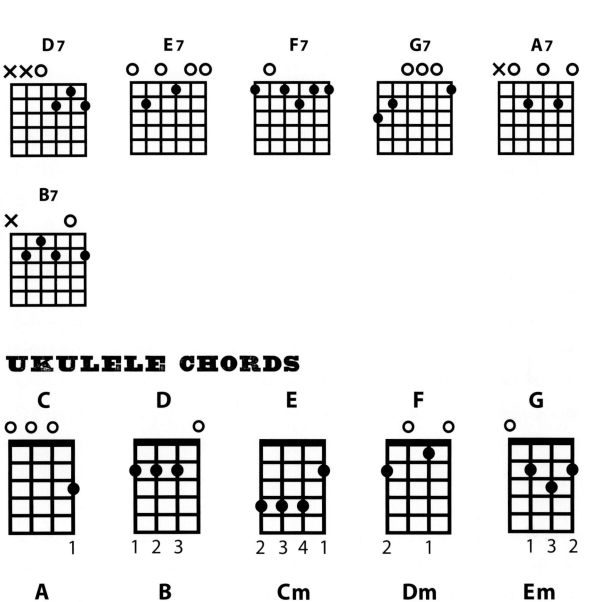

UKULELE CHORDS

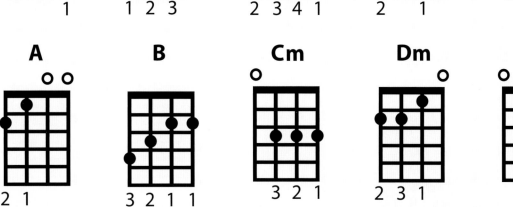

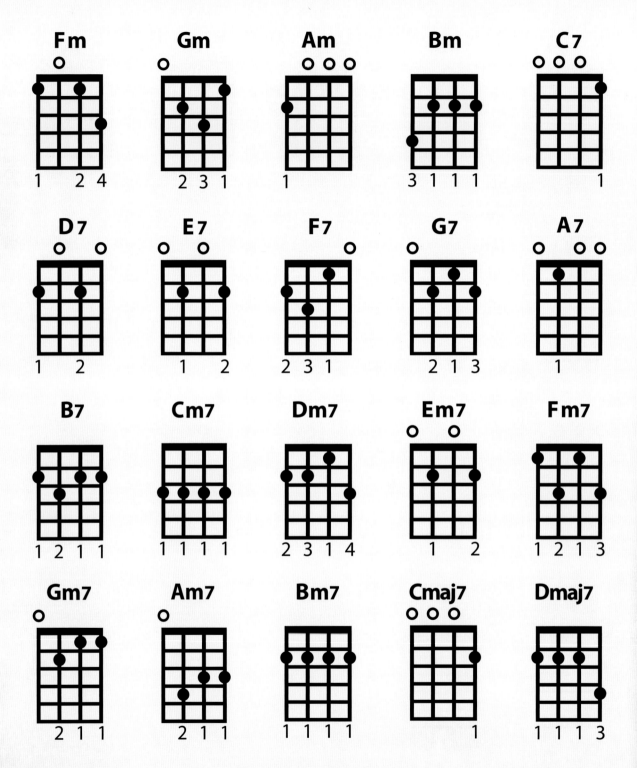

INDEX

ACKNOWLEDGMENTS

I've been collaborating with Donald Saaf since the initial recording ("Over the Rainbow") for what became the first family CD (*Rocket Ship Beach*). He's influenced the sound and the look of this musical universe in more ways that I can count. We've always talked about someday making a songbook and I'm so grateful that after almost twenty years of music-making we finally had the chance.

These songs didn't just land in my head. Many, many people have taken the time to introduce me, directly and indirectly, to the tunes you'll find in the book. I'm grateful for their friendship and inspiration: Tareq Abboushi, The Villa-Lobos Brothers, Jose Joaquin Garcia, David Jones, Lead Belly, The Johnson Girls, The New York Packet, Mario DeVolcy, Tony Saletan, Aggie Decaul, Rosita Isles, Patsy Primus, Sally Reece, Georgia Bryan, Wayne Rhoden a.k.a. Father Goose, Carl Sandburg, Mike Seeger, Pete Seeger, Taoufiq Ben Amor, Liz Mitchell and Daniel Littleton, Caridad de la Luz a.k.a. La Bruja, Cumbiamba eNeYe, Sonia de los Santos, Bernardo Palombo, Basya Schechter, Gaston "Bonga" Jean-Baptiste, Frankie and Dougy Quimby, The Children of Agape, and Elena Moon Park.

What is a song without the singers and players who make it come alive? As I look at this list of collaborators I'm extremely humbled to think that I've had the opportunity to share musical space with them all. Without the stratospheric contributions of the following people my records would be the sound of a guy alone in a room trying to tune his guitar: Barbara Brousal, Cary Tamarkin, John Dinicola, Alyssa Lamb, Cynthia Hopkins, David Hilliard, Colin Brooks, Yoshi Waki, George Rush, Sheryl Crow, Suzanne Vega, Simon Kirke, G. E. Smith, Marc Ribler, Rosanne Cash, The Rubí Theater Company, Sandra Bernhard, Lyris Hung, Yuriana Sobrino, Loudon Wainwright III, Aimee Mann, Nell Campbell, Lou Reed, Dar Williams, John Doe, Bob Weir, Angelique Kidjo, Debbie Harry, Courin Gibbs, David Jones, Philip Glass, Toshi Reagon, The Sullivan Family, The Mockler Family, Marc Ribot, Silvia Sierra, Joaquin M. Del Rosario, Isidro Chavez, Lila Downs, Daphne Rubin-Vega, Sharon Jones, Andrew Bird, Joan Osborne, The Sierra Leone Refugee All-Stars, Shawana Kemp a.k.a. Shine, Carol Channing, Derick K. Grant, Brian Stokes Mitchell, de'Adre Aziza, Matthew Broderick, John Foti, Pat Irwin, The Blind Boys of Alabama, Natalie Merchant, The Kronos Quartet, Wunmi, Nick Cave, Roy Nathanson, Curtis Folkes, Patrick Dougher, Simi Stone, Jerry Marotta, Rachelle Garniez, Billy Bragg, Chuck D., Memphis Jelks, Steve Uhrick, Rebecca Naomi Jones, Saskia Lane, Charlie Faye, Julian Crouch, Dominic James, Isak and Ole Saaf, Madame Marie Jean Laurent, Ceddyjay, Aloe Blacc, Shareef Swindell, Tamar Kali, Little Goose, Pauline Jean, Valerie June, Ashley Phillips, Marley Reedy, Neha Jiwrajka, and Jendog Lonewolf.

I'd like to thank Astrid Lewis Reedy for many years of beautiful design, great advice, inspiration, enthusiasm, and friendship. They wouldn't have been the same without her direction.

These songs have all appeared on Festival Five Records, the independent label I started in 2000. Without the guidance, support, friendship, and expert advice of Peter Wright and his crew at Vitual Label, the train would have run off the tracks years ago.

I hope that you all have a chance to listen to the records that I've made over the years. Rob Friedman has been my patiently inspired co-producer on all of them and I can't imagine creating this catalog without him.

Thank you to my long-suffering, musically minded editor Dennis Pernu. He called me with the idea for this book and, although I'm sure there were many times he must have felt like it was a tragic mistake, I'm so grateful that he brought the idea to the good people of Quarto Publishing Group and rallied for the incredible support that I've received. No Dennis, no House Party! I thank everyone at Quarto for their dedication and commitment to this book. I am particularly grateful to James Kegley, Alyssa Lochner, Laura Drew, Erik Gilg, Onalee Smith, and Ken Fund. Special thanks, too, to Rita Farah of Justice Page Middle School in Minneapolis for her translation help with "Salaam."

I'd also like to thank, Hope Butterworth Zanes, Julia Zanes, Warren Zanes, Akaya Windwood, Mike Feldstein, Rae Lynn Ambach, Simon Shaw, Sherri Leathers and everyone at Shaw Entertainment, Linda Brumbach and Alisa Regas and everyone at Pomegranate Arts, The Lead Belly Family and Estate, John Reynolds, Brooklyn Music School, The Herman Family and Camp Interlocken (now Windsor Mountain), Betty Siegel, Roger Ideishi, and the TYA crew at The Kennedy Center, Brian MacDevitt, Bill and Dr. Bob, Paula Greif, Annie Leibovitz, Judy Mcgrath, Yolanda Cuomo, Stephanie Mayers, Irene Cabrera, Rachel Chanoff, John Allen, Jeff Place, Mary Monseur, Huib Shippers, John Smith, Cecile Chen, Beshu Gedamu, Fred Knittel, Atesh Sonneborn and everyone at Smithsonian Folkways.

Thank you to Billy Buss for tireless early-morning and late-night assistance with the notation in this book. In his other life, Billy is a dedicated music teacher and well-known jazz trumpeter. Find out more at billybuss.com

None of this would have happened if my daughter Anna hadn't asked me to play some music at her birthday party way back when. She's been my constant inspiration and tireless cheerleader and I feel blessed to have her in my life!

The music in this book represents the best of my past. The music I make with my wife, Claudia Eliaza, is my musical future. I dedicate this to her.

I'm thankful to God for my musical life and for the opportunity to make this book.

—Dan Zanes
Brooklyn, NY
July 2018

For Julia, Isak, Ole, Sylvia, Captain, and Snufkin.

—Donald Saaf
Brattleboro, VT
July 2018

CLAUDIA SAYS "THANK YOU" TOO!

I would like to thank God, first and foremost, for the gift of music that has been a constant in her life; my parents, Claude and Paulette Eliaza; my brother Jonathan for always supporting my musical pursuits; my music mentors Emily Gates, Jamie Shew, and Bill and Robyn Brawley for affording me so many different opportunities to create and share music; the Community Music Center of Boston; my Music Therapist posse, Kimberly Khare, Karen Wacks, Caryl Beth Thomas, Lorrie Kubicek, and Samantha Hale, for the incredible mentorship and supervision; my dear friends Mike Clifford, Mandalyn Meades, Attis Clopton, Pauline Jean, Godwin Louis, James White, and Sally Haines for love, support, and friendship that knows no bounds; my Haitian brothers and sisters near and far; all of the beautiful, inspiring families and participants that I've had the honor of working with in music therapy sessions over the years; and last but certainly not least, my incredible husband, Dan Zanes, who teaches me on a daily basis what it means to love fully and freely. You inspire me more than you know.

—Claudia Eliaza
Brooklyn, NY
July 2018

ROCK ISLAND LINE
New Words and New Music Arrangement by Huddie Ledbetter
Edited and new additional material by Alan Lomax
TRO-© Copyright 1959 (Renewed) Folkways Music Publishers, Inc., New York, NY
International Copyright Secured   Made in U.S.A.
All Rights Reserved Including Public Performance for Profit
Used by Permission

SO GLAD I'M HERE
Written and Adapted by Bessie Jones
Collected and Edited by Alan Lomax
TRO-© Copyright 2016 Ludlow Music, Inc., New York, NY
International Copyright Secured   Made in U.S.A.
All Rights Reserved Including Public Performance for Profit
Used by Permission

SWEET ROSYANNE
Words and Music by The Bright Light Quartette (Lawrence Hodge, Arnold Fisher, James Campbell, Robert Beane and Shedrick Caine) and Alan Lomax
TRO-© Copyright 1966 (Renewed) 1975 (Renewed) Ludlow Music, Inc., New York, NY
International Copyright Secured   Made in U.S.A.
All Rights Reserved Including Public Performance for Profit
Used by Permission

TURN! TURN! TURN! (The Children's Version)
Words from the Book of Ecclesiastes
Adaptation and Music by Pete Seeger
New words by Toshi Seeger
TRO-© Copyright 1962 (Renewed) and 1990 Melody Trails, Inc., New York, NY
International Copyright Secured   Made in U.S.A.
All Rights Reserved Including Public Performance for Profit
Used by Permission

Page 14, Bessie Jones photo by Diana Davies, courtesy of Ralph Rinzler Archives and Collections, Smithsonian Institution. Page 33, Ruth Crawford Seeger photo courtesy Library of Congress. Page 64, Dr. Bernice Reagon Johnson photo by Diana Davies, courtesy of Ralph Rinzler Archives and Collections, Smithsonian Institution. Page 96, Ella Jenkins photo courtesy Ella Jenkins and Smithsonian Folkways Recordings. Page 124, José-Luis Orozco photo by Daniel E. Sheehy, courtesy Smithsonian Folkways Recordings.